Origins of the English

DUCKWORTH DEBATES IN ARCHAEOLOGY

Series editor: Richard Hodges

Also available

Archaeology and Text
John Moreland

Beyond Celts, Germans and Scythians
Peter S. Wells

Debating the Archaeological Heritage
Robin Skeates

Loot, Legitimacy and Ownership
Colin Renfrew

Towns and Trade in the Age of Charlemagne
Richard Hodges

Origins of the English

Catherine Hills

Duckworth

This impression 2006
First published in 2003
Gerald Duckworth & Co. Ltd.
90-93 Cowcross Street, London EC1M 6BF
Tel: 020 7490 7300
Fax: 020 7490 0080
inquiries@duckworth-publishers.co.uk
www.ducknet.co.uk

A catalogue record for this book is available
from the British Library

ISBN 0 7156 3191 8

Contents

Acknowledgements

I am grateful to Richard Hodges for asking me to write this book, to Deborah Blake at Duckworth for being patient while I wrote it, and to my family, especially Henry, for being even more patient and forbearing. I would also like to thank colleagues, both at Cambridge and elsewhere, who have inspired or informed me through their writings or in discussion, and Sam Lucy who read and commented on a draft of the text. I am also grateful to Aleks Pluskowski for producing the map. Above all, this book owes a great deal to my students, especially the graduates whose PhD theses I have supervised, advised on, or examined. These contain more comprehensive and critical discussion of most of the topics in this book than can be found in published works, including this one.

Cambridge C.M.H.
2002

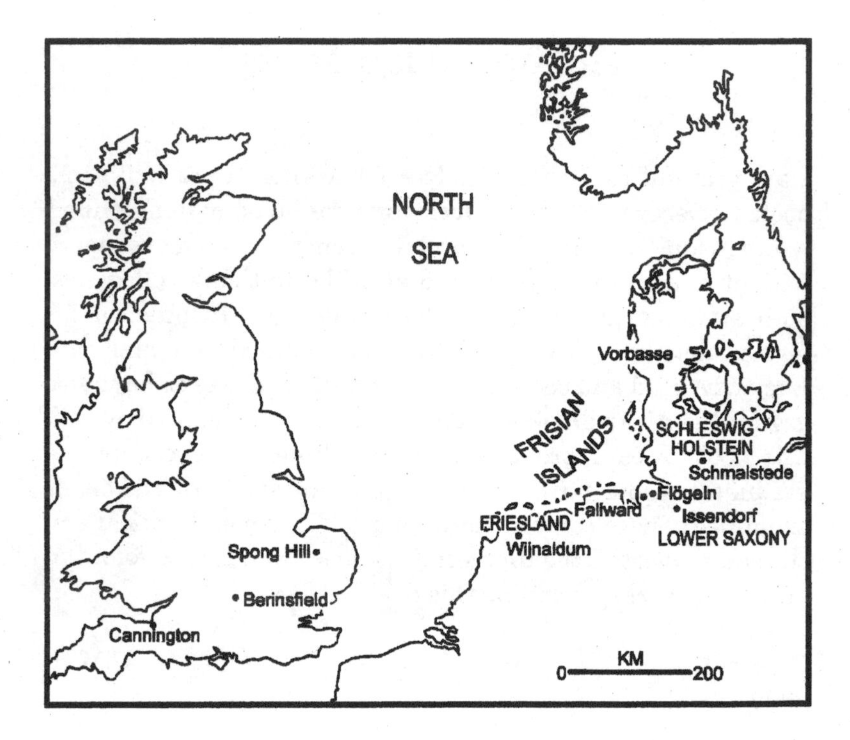
NORTH
SEA
Vorbasse
FRISIAN
ISLANDS
SCHLESWIG
HOLSTEIN
Schmalstede
Flögeln
Fallward
Issendorf
FRIESLAND
Wijnaldum
LOWER SAXONY
Spong Hill
Berinsfield
Cannington
KM
0
200

1

Introduction

There are at least three logical starting points for a discussion of English origins. One is around ten thousand years ago, when people first recolonised this north-western corner of the Eurasian landmass after the last Ice Age. A second is the tenth century AD, when the descendants of King Alfred created a single political entity, England, from a series of smaller Anglo-Saxon and Scandinavian kingdoms.

Both have considerable logic and simplicity in their favour as starting points. I have, however, chosen to concentrate on the third, the fifth century AD, the period which saw the transition from Roman Britain to Anglo-Saxon England. Most accounts of the early history of Britain describe how, after the disintegration of the western Roman empire in the early fifth century, the south and east of the country was overrun by Germanic peoples, the Anglo-Saxons, who came from what is now northern Germany and southern Scandinavia. The native population was killed, driven westwards, or enslaved, so that the later inhabitants of southern and eastern Britain are descended from the new arrivals, who became the English, speaking the English language and occupying the part of Britain called after them, England.

This story fits into a pattern of writing early history, and of explaining national identity, which has existed since ancient historians first identified different peoples. A nation has an identity, defined in terms of territory, language, religion, material culture and ethnicity, all of which are seen as having their ultimate source, and justification, in the past. At some stage in the past each people, already defined as a separate group, came from somewhere else to their present territory, which has been theirs to hold and rule against all others ever since. It is possible, however, to question this method of explanation both in general terms and specifically in relation to the English. There are other ways in which national identity can be created.

A long time ago I was a student travelling overland to Greece to do archaeological fieldwork. We drove across Yugoslavia, in those days a strange and alien place, part of the dangerous Eastern Bloc. Oxen drew ploughs across open fields, like the pictures in medieval manuscripts, and in the cities very old women in black dug tiny plots within the walls of ruined buildings. Everyone spoke only Serbo-Croat and eyed us with deep suspicion (as did the British School in Athens when we got there, but that is another story). Fast-forward to 2002, and a trip with my own students to Croatia. This is a beautiful country with a long history and spectacular archaeological monuments, explained to us by a series of erudite and charming Croatian archaeologists, nearly all in perfect English. On the way home we came to the border between Croatia and Slovenia. This is a frontier of the type seldom encountered in western Europe these days, complete with border posts manned by police and uniformed officials who just might decide to take your vehicle apart. Croatia and Slovenia have different languages and money which cannot easily be exchanged. But when I drove across Yugoslavia neither had a separate existence – most adult Croatians and Slovenians were born Yugoslavian (except for the Slovenian archaeologist we met who turned out to be originally English, a former student). Of course there is a long and tangled history behind the events of recent years; Croatia did not come from nowhere in 1991. The point I want to make here is simply that people can change their names, language, currency and political allegiance without the majority of the population being replaced.

The traditional kind of historical explanation still has deadly power, but in reality we can see that it has seldom if ever been so simple, whether in the part of the Balkans where Yugoslavia existed in the second half of the twentieth century, or in Britain in the fifth century AD. The reason that events recorded in the latter period still attract interest and dispute is because they relate to modern British identities: are the English, Scots and Welsh different peoples, or are they simply subdivisions of the same underlying British population? Did the English arrive as an intrusive band of invaders and migrants, planting themselves in eastern Britain and replacing earlier populations? Or was it a change in political allegiance that changed Britons to Anglo-Saxons? In which case any differences between the English, Welsh and Scots (and of course Irish, but there is not space in this book to include Ireland) are the cumulative result of their histories, separate or united, and not caused by any intrinsic racial distinction.

We are in fact much less sure than we used to be as to how south-east Britain became England. Engaging with the issues raised by this debate involves looking at the ways in which we understand historical and archaeological evidence and use them in the construction of identity, using this as a case study to explore issues which have much wider relevance.

The context of debate

Discussion has often been set within very limited confines, divided into narrow slots of time and space. Separate specialists have studied Roman and early medieval Britain, Anglo-Saxons and Britons, and they do not always communicate with each other, or look far outside the geographical and chronological frontiers of their own special knowledge. It is very easy to present a story of the rise, decline and fall of a whole series of aspects of a society, or its material culture, set within the neat limits of our own chosen time and place of study. But that time and place is a part of a much larger continuum. Concentrating only on one's own back yard in this way can give very odd results. Too many distribution maps stop at modern political frontiers, which to the unwary may suggest they were ancient frontiers, whereas in fact the pattern is a product of the practicalities of modern research. We may have plotted every brooch within our own territory, but if we do not know where else, and when, they occur – or are really absent – the map will not tell us very much. And although it is useful to study fourth-century 'Roman' pottery and metalwork as a source for motifs and styles taken up and developed later in 'Germanic' material, it is upside-down logic to describe the fourth-century material as therefore 'Germanic' and to see its distribution as indicating where early settlers lived, rather than locating it within the continuing development of style and production within the Roman world.

Another kind of time depth relates to scholarship. Each generation knows, and criticises, the work of its immediate predecessors, but is less familiar with, and even more dismissive of, older research (except where it seems to fit well with 'new' arguments). So we do not realise that our present views, far from being startlingly original, are in fact part of a continuing debate. Nor do we always see where our own work fits within contemporary debate, our ideas partly – though not entirely – shaped by our intellectual and academic background. We also tend to simplify other scholars' research, and to pigeonhole them as representing a particular line of thought, although most of us would admit (at least privately) to changing our own minds, to indecision, or even to holding contradictory views at the same time.

Research into the early history of Britain involves specialists from many different disciplines: historians, archaeologists, linguists, philologists, botanists, osteologists and geneticists – and more, especially since archaeology is such an eclectic discipline that there are few subjects it has not drawn on. But despite sustained attempts, real interdisciplinary dialogue is rare because it is extremely difficult. From our earliest schooldays we are trained to see academic boundaries and to stay within them, and in practical terms very few if any of us are able to master the detail of more than one subject, and usually only a small part of that. Each of us is well aware of the limitations and subtleties of evidence within our own field and able to assess the validity of arguments presented by colleagues. But from other disciplines we take on trust results produced by techniques we cannot master ourselves. There is no easy way round this, and it is after all how most of us acquire knowledge on most subjects – how many of us really have first-hand experience or detailed understanding of most of what we 'know' about the world? What we can and should attempt to do is to look critically at the interface between our results and those of others. We should be particularly aware of the danger of using conclusions which might have been queried or superseded in another discipline as frameworks for our own detailed research. The venerable Bede claimed (in the eighth century) that the Picts came from Scythia – but we need to try to define what he understood by 'Scythia' and why he made this claim. A geneticist studying Scotland should not fall into the trap of seeing this statement as good reason to look for connections between Scottish and Russian populations. Similarly, as archaeologists we probably should not imagine that there is an Anglo-Saxon gene which might be easily extracted from ancient skeletons. We need to enter into better dialogue with each other, and be willing to explain the premises on which we have based our complex structures. Sometimes we may have to admit we have built on sand. As an archaeologist I cannot attempt to assess the validity of results achieved by techniques I have not mastered, such as philology or genetics, but I can explore the ways in which those results have been interpreted, especially in relation to conclusions drawn from archaeological research.

Names

The very name 'English' needs further explanation. The earliest historical references, in classical sources from outside Britain, refer to piratical Germanic raiders, 'Saxones', who attacked the shores of Britannia and Gaul in the third century AD and stimulated the construction of a strong defence system. After Britain ceased to be part of the Roman empire, occasional references to Britain in continental sources portray it as subject to raids and conquest by people most often still called Saxons. The earliest British sources also refer to Saxons, and this name was in general taken up by British neighbours and enemies, hence 'Sassenach'. So why did south Britain not become Saxony? As early as the sixth century, Procopius, writing in Constantinople, knew of three different peoples, Britons, Frisians and Angles, living in what had by then become a remote and unfamiliar land to the surviving eastern Roman empire, while in the eighth century Bede famously described the arrival of the Angles, Saxons and Jutes. Both include Angles and Saxons, the basis for the hybrid 'Anglo-Saxon'. It has been argued that the Christian Church was influential in the eventual dominance of the name Angle over Saxon (Wormald 1983). In the sixth century, Pope Gregory saw slaves for sale in the market place in Rome. Struck by their beauty, he asked where they came from. On being told they were Angles he remarked, 'Non Angli sed angeli', and decided forthwith to send missionaries to convert these angelic, but heathen, people. In the eighth century Bede included this story in his history of the church of the English (not Saxon) people, the *Historia Ecclesiastica Gentis Anglorum*.

Other eighth-century writers, including Boniface, a Saxon, also referred to the English people (behaving badly when abroad) so this was not a usage confined to the Anglians. So when in the ninth century the West Saxon king Alfred referred to his people as 'Angelcynn', and their language as 'Englisc', he was following an established practice. It is no accident that the English call themselves by the name sanctified by the Church as that of a people chosen by God, whereas their enemies use the name originally applied to piratical raiders.

Identities

Names relate to identities, which can be defined in many different ways, but which most of us validate by reference to origins. Knowing where we come from, as individuals and as members of societies, seems to give that identity a secure foundation. But identity, whether collective or individual, is a complex subject. All of us have multiple identities, as members of families, genders, age-groups, religions and professions, and as inhabitants of streets, towns, regions, countries and continents. Most of those identities are definable for most people through fairly simple and uncontentious criteria. This is not true for race, ethnicity or nationality, which, as we know only too well, are the source of continuing bloodshed. Each of us knows which ethnic group or nation we believe ourselves to belong to, although this may not remain the same throughout our lives. We also think we know what the literal and metaphorical place of that group in the world is or should be – but others do not always agree with us.

There is often disagreement on the defining characteristics that demarcate one group of people from another, and many of the claimed differences can be argued not to have an objective existence outside the minds of those who believe in them. But that belief can be extremely powerful. What or who people think they are themselves is probably the only real basis for definition, but most of us prefer to claim external validation for our identity. Justification is sought especially in the past, and historical, linguistic, archaeological and genetic evidence is deployed to demonstrate that one set of people is and always has been different from another. From this it is a short step for each group to define itself as superior, with legitimate reasons for attacking others who can be redefined as intrinsically less important or deserving – or even less human. But although history may explain, it does not really justify or legitimate. We should look for the origins of conflict not in some externally defined set of events in the past for which we can blame someone else, but across the whole range of past and present relationships between individuals and societies, and between humans and their environment.

For centuries, however, histories have been written on the basis that peoples are definable entities. A recurrent powerful theme is the story of a people who came from one place to another. For western Europe the most powerful model for this is the biblical story of the Israelites and the Promised Land. There might be disagreement in detail – were the inhabitants of Britain Britons who had come from Troy with Brutus, or Angles, Saxons and Jutes who had arrived with Hengest? But the principle is the same – the assumption that a people is identifiable and distinct, and that it came at some distant time in the past from somewhere else to its proper present home. To some extent this is intrinsic to biblical history, since the Old Testament account of the descent of all people from Adam and Eve – and indeed from Noah after the Flood – implies that their descendants must have spread out and moved into the rest of the world from an original homeland. This underlies not only early history but also, until recently, most archaeological interpretation of prehistory. It is not so different in principle from the current account of the origin of modern humans in Africa and their spread to the rest of the world. Ultimately, however, it is not a satisfactory explanatory device for movements after initial colonisation because it does not explain how, when or why separate peoples were created, nor why they set out on their travels. They simply emerge from a mythical past fully fledged as a definable group. It also makes assumptions about the distinctiveness of separate peoples which we now see as debatable, for the reasons given above. But it is so deeply rooted that calling it in question, as archaeologists have done now for some decades, still provokes considerable opposition, as witness the current debate about the Celts (James 1998; Sims-Williams 1998b). I myself have been accused of calling the Venerable Bede a liar simply for suggesting that his version of events, however learned and well informed he undoubtedly was, might not be the only possible account.

Most countries in western Europe draw on three different traditions in writing their own histories: native, classical and Christian. Which is given greater emphasis, and the extent to which they are seen as alternative or complementary to each other, varies according to the author's perspective. In Britain, native sources include both British and Germanic, and a variety of changing relationships with the classical world and Christianity are reflected in the use of sources.

The period commonly thought to be crucial in this discussion is the fifth century AD, when the western Roman empire disintegrated into a network of warring territories, many of them ruled by the leaders of Germanic peoples from outside the empire, such as the Franks in the Rhineland and northern France, the Ostrogoths in Italy, and the Anglo-Saxons in Britain. Saxons are recorded from the third century AD among pirates troubling the east coast of Britain, and are seen as arriving in force as invaders and settlers during the fifth century. The traditional account of this 'Adventus Saxonum' suggests they arrived at a date calculated by Bede in the eighth century as AD 449. This is one of three apparently pivotal dates in the early history of Britain, the others being the arrival of the Romans in AD 43 and the invasion of William the Conqueror in 1066. In popular perception the clock seems to have been set to zero at each of these dates, minimising the contribution made by all previous inhabitants and undermining serious interest in prehistory: if the prehistoric peoples of Britain were successively replaced we are not descended from them, they do not form part of our roots, and they can safely be put aside as curiosities who left strange stone monuments we can visit on days out. In his *History of Britain* series on television, Simon Schama covered the four thousand years before the Norman Conquest in a single programme, but devoted another whole programme to that event. However, even those who see 1066 as the starting point for all subsequent political and cultural development in Britain do not argue that it saw dramatic change in the basic population, only in the ruling class. The arrival of the Anglo-Saxons, by contrast, is still perceived as an important and interesting event because it is believed to have been a key factor in the evolution of the identity of the present inhabitants of the British Isles, involving migration on such a scale as to permanently change the population of south-east Britain, and making the English a distinct and different people from the Celtic Irish, Welsh and Scots.

One reason for exploring the origins of the English is because their identity matters not only to those who identify themselves as English but also to all the other peoples with whom the English have, and have had, relationships of all kinds. Another is that this is an example of a national origin myth which throws light (or perhaps darkness) on all such myths, and shows why there are seldom simple answers to questions about origins. It also relates to a key period in the history of Europe. The disintegration, or transformation, of the western Roman empire during the fifth century AD led to the creation of a series of kingdoms from which emerged the nation states of Europe, including Britain. Despite the existence of the European Union, the peoples of Europe are still very well aware of their national differences, and concerned to explain and account for them.

The simple version of the story is that the English arrived in Britain during the fifth century AD as immigrants and invaders from North Germany. The Anglo-Saxons crossed the North Sea in force, overwhelmed and destroyed the British population, who no longer had the Roman army to defend them, and occupied southern and eastern Britain. From that time onwards the English have been racially distinct from the other peoples of the British Isles – the Scots and the Welsh – who are descended from the native Britons who survived in the north and west, and who are also related to the Irish. Briton or Celt can thus be separated from Anglo-Saxon English.

An alternative view plays down the size and significance of the invading force, and allows much of the British population to survive even in eastern Britain. In this version, the English are largely descended from the Britons and are not racially distinct from the other inhabitants of the British Isles. The implications of this are clear: all those who believe, often very strongly, in the difference between Celt and English, have an easy justification and explanation for that difference in the traditional invasion and replacement account. If that is not what happened, different arguments will be needed.

Different interpretations of the fifth century are also important in terms of attitudes to more recent immigrants. If there are 'pure' Celtic and Anglo-Saxon peoples, distinct and separate from each other, then both might also be distinct from other groups who have arrived since the fifth century. If, however, Romans, Anglo-Saxons, Danes and Normans, while conquering parts of the British Isles and adding to its population stock, modified but did not replace the existing population, then a 'mongrel' race is what we have had for the past two thousand years, and more recent immigration is simply a continuation of that process. Strongly held ideological views therefore contribute to the perpetuation of one or other version of history. This has always been true, and in the next chapter I shall outline the changing attitudes to the Anglo-Saxons which have influenced accounts of their arrival and impact on Britain.[1]

2

Attitudes to Anglo-Saxons

Rather than starting with an account of the evidence and what it might tell us, I shall give here a brief account of the history of attitudes towards the Anglo-Saxons from their first appearance in historical accounts to the present.[1] The changes in perspective are clearly as much, or more, contingent on contemporary political and religious ideology as on any kind of evidence. This remains true today. The same material is interpreted differently according to the background of the interpreter. There are significant divisions between prehistorians, classicists and medievalists, between historians, linguists and archaeologists, between geneticists and osteologists, between those with a more insular or a more European outlook, between generations of scholars, and between individuals. Two recent books on late Roman Britain, both written by relatively young male British scholars, use much of the same evidence to arrive at very different conclusions. For one the fourth century was a 'Golden Age', whereas for the other it was a time of oppression and decline (de la Bédoyère 1999; Faulkner 2000). One has focussed on the lifestyle of the well-to-do – villas, mosaics, sculpture, and evidence for art and literature – while the other has looked at the run-down state of towns and the tax burdens imposed on the peasantry. Neither is exclusively right or wrong, and both have interesting things to say. It is quite easy to see, and perhaps partly explain, the differences here. In other cases it is more subtle, but it is essential to try to locate scholarship in its own time and mental landscape before assessing what it really has to tell us.

The history of Anglo-Saxon studies is a striking example of the ways in which knowledge is embedded in the society which produces it. There are recurrent themes in this history which can perhaps be grouped under three headings. The first is destiny: the Anglo-Saxons seen as fulfilling God's purpose or, later, the laws of historical progress. Secondly, Rome cast a long shadow. The Roman empire could be claimed as ancestral to Britain, presented as a role model to be emulated and surpassed, or downgraded in favour of a purer Teutonic ancestry. Finally, the relationships between the different peoples of Britain and between Britain and Europe continue to give the subject its force. There has usually been a dominant version of the story, but always dissentient voices as well.

Even the names given to the period which begins in the middle of the first millennium AD show how differently it can be viewed, and indicate the priorities of those using them. The choice of terminology for chronological periods and the societies which existed in them reveals each author's view of their defining aspects and often shapes their interpretation. There are three main types of name, essentially the same three as those used in the construction of historical narrative. Some refer back to the Roman empire, some to Christianity, and some to ruling dynasties or peoples, mostly Germanic.

'The Dark Ages', still current in popular terminology, was coined to describe the period which seemed to lie between the extinguishing of the light of the classical world with the fall of the Roman empire, and the rebirth of civilisation with the rediscovery of classical literature in the Renaissance. Most medievalists, understandably, dislike this as a name for the period they study. It is imprecise and value-laden, suggesting both that we do not know much about the period, and that the people of that time were all ignorant and uncivilised, neither of which is true. It is certainly not 'dark' compared to most of prehistory, nor was the break between Roman and medieval complete or sudden. Other names also refer to the Roman world: 'late antique', 'post-Roman' and 'sub-Roman'. Even 'medieval' and 'Middle Ages' depend on a tripartite division between the ancient classical world, the modern world, and a period in the middle. Names relating to religion are less often used than they once were, but 'early Christian' is still a fairly common term in the British Isles, together with 'the pagan period', and 'the conversion period' in England.

The movement of peoples has often been seen as they key factor in what has consequently been called 'the migration period' in several languages, of which the German 'Völkerwanderungszeit' is the most widely used. Political authority is represented by the names of the successive Frankish Merovingian and Carolingian dynasties, sometimes used outside the areas where they actually held power (e.g. Merovingian in Norway). Outside the former Roman empire in Scandinavia the first millennium AD is not perceived as divided into separate slices by Rome, and 'the Iron Age' is used, divided into 'Roman' and 'Germanic' (with many further subdivisions, some defined by art styles) until 'the Vikings' take over around 800. Within Britain, the names of peoples are sometimes applied to chronology – the Pictish period in Scotland, for example. In England, 'Anglo-Saxon' predominates as a name for the period from the mid-fifth century to 1066, with a northern modification to Anglian and Anglo-Scandinavian. A common usage is to sub-divide between early, middle and late Saxon – defined by arrival, conversion, Vikings and Norman conquest. All these names carry mental baggage. The more abbreviated and apparently neutral they become (especially prevalent in archaeological labelling) – ERIA, LRIA, ES, MS, LS – the more embedded and uncritically accepted are the concepts they embody. It would be better to use simple chronological terms (although, of course, AD is itself a powerful ideological term), and I shall do that where possible.

In this chapter my concern is with attitudes towards the Anglo-Saxons, not the validity of sources as historical evidence. It is not always easy to discover what those attitudes were, since we are reading texts now with our very different understanding of the world from that of their authors. The words themselves, even when we think they are accurately translated, did not have the same associations in the past as those we give them now. This is especially problematic in connection with words for groupings of peoples which have accumulated historical and modern meanings. If we translate *gens*, *populus* or *natio* as 'tribe', 'people' or 'nation', we may be importing meanings to the text which were not in the mind of the original author. Even apparently simple words, such as *urbs* : town; *ecclesia* : church, evoke a very different image for us from that which would have been in the mind of a north European medieval monk.

How have these 'English' been perceived by those who have written accounts of their origins and later history? The initial classical sources are hostile references to marauding pirates. Medieval accounts from within Britain survive in works written usually by Christian clerics. What they say must always be understood in the context of explicit or implicit Christian messages. It often needs to be interpreted either as a sophisticated analogy with events in the Bible or as a location of the history of Britain within the framework of a biblical and/or classical past, rather than as a straightforward objective narrative.

The earliest and most influential narrative account of the Anglo-Saxon arrival in Britain was written at some date between the late fifth and the mid-sixth centuries AD by a British cleric known as Gildas (Winterbottom 1978; Lapidge and Dumville 1984; Higham 1994). His polemic against contemporary British rulers includes an account of the violent invasion of Britain by ferocious Saxons. According to Gildas, they were unwisely invited in as defence against other enemies, the Picts and Scots, but turned against their hosts and pillaged the island. The remnant of the native population eventually rallied and fought back, winning the battle of Mount Badon under a leader unnamed by Gildas but often subsequently called Arthur. This was in the year of Gildas' birth, forty-four years before the time he was writing, which would be a more useful chronological framework if we knew either date. The decades on either side of 500 is really as precise a date as we can give.

Gildas gives a dramatic picture of invasion and destruction, which has been deployed ever since. He was not, however, attempting to write objective history; he wrote as a biblical prophet calling the rulers of his day to repentance. God would punish them for their wickedness, he said, as he had punished their predecessors through the Saxon invasions. He describes the destruction of cities, in ruins to his own day, the people dead or in flight, unburied corpses and congealed blood. Even so, not everyone was killed, since by Gildas' own day the Britons were numerous and prosperous enough to indulge in the sins which caused his complaints. Much ink has been spilt on the precise date and location of Gildas' own life and the events he records. What he does clearly tell us is that Germanic peoples invaded Britain during the fifth century and caused great destruction but not, at least by the time and in the region of Britain where Gildas was writing (whenever and wherever that was), the complete annihilation of the native population, or even of classical learning or Christianity – since he himself had clearly been educated in the classical tradition and as a Christian.

Anglo-Saxon ideas about themselves and their origins come to us through the writings of scholarly Christian clerics who wrote many years after the migration. The first and greatest of these was Bede (*c.* 672-735), a monk at Jarrow who completed his *Ecclesiastical History of the English People* in 731 (Colgrave and Mynors 1969). This work remains so influential that it is still difficult to construct any alternative to his account of the early Anglo-Saxon period.

Bede uses Gildas and neatly turns the British author's view of the invaders as the instruments of divine wrath to perception of the Anglo-Saxons as a people chosen by God, like the Israelites. Bede tells us that the Anglo-Saxons came from three powerful Germanic tribes, the Angles, Saxons and Jutes. He locates these tribes on the continent and after settlement within England in terms of the political geography and nomenclature of his own day: the Saxons came from Saxony and from them descended the East, South and West Saxons of Bede's day. The Angles were from 'Angeln', the land between the Jutes and the Saxons, and they were ancestral to the East and Middle Angles, the Mercians and 'all who dwell north of the Humber', while the Jutes, from Jutland, settled in Kent, the Isle of Wight and part of Hampshire. An important point to remember about Bede and later medieval writers is that the society he knew was hierarchical, and the ancestry and deeds of the aristocracy, whether kings or saints, was what mattered. A lord's people were his followers – warriors who were attracted to successful leaders – and also those who lived on the lands he ruled. The genealogy of kings was recorded; that of the peasants tilling the soil was not. It was important to belong to the local powerful group and to define yourself as a member of it, to be recognised and to see yourself as an Anglo-Saxon in lands ruled by kings who traced their ancestry back to the Germanic god Woden. But whether most of the population acquired that identity through descent or through their rulers was not a question explored by early writers, probably because it did not seem of as much importance to them as it does to us.

Anglo-Saxons and Britons did think they were separate peoples. The ninth-century work known as the *Historia Brittonum*, 'written in Wales by a multi-lingual cleric' (Dumville 1985, p. 3), lists four peoples as inhabiting Britain: the Britons themselves, the Gaels, the Picts and the English, each of whom had arrived at times in the past, calculated in relation to biblical chronology. There were legal distinctions in some Anglo-Saxon lawcodes: compensation for injury or crime (*wergild*) was set at a lower rate for Welshmen than Anglo-Saxons, although the name for Welshman, *wealh*, only later acquired the secondary meaning 'slave' (Faull 1975). Anglo-Saxons believed themselves to be related to the continental Saxons, and a motivating force behind their missionary enterprise to the continent in the eighth century was to bring their pagan cousins into the Christian Church. The English missionary Boniface wrote that the German Saxons themselves believed that they were of one blood and bone with the English (Whitelock 1968, p. 748).

The story of the arrival of the Anglo-Saxons was preserved in royal genealogies which trace the ancestry of kings back to Germanic gods and heroes, and also to biblical figures. These were political documents, constructed and adapted at various stages to strengthen the position of rulers who wanted to legitimate power (which may often have been recently established through force) by appealing to ancestral authority (Dumville 1977b). Stories were told about the heroic founders of the dynasties of which we now have only hints, recorded chiefly in the Anglo-Saxon Chronicle. This complex set of documents was compiled at different times and in different places. The earliest written version was produced in Wessex, probably in the reign of King Alfred (871-99), while the last entries in one version were as late as 1154 (Swanton 1996). The early entries cannot be used at face value, although they clearly do embody traditions about events in the fifth and sixth centuries. The *Historia Brittonum* includes the stories about Hengest, given Kent by the British king Vortigern who was besotted with Hengest's daughter, and about Arthur and Mount Badon, all of which have since formed the basis of what most people think they know about the period. These accounts have in common a focus on leaders and their followers and on warfare. Ordinary people appear only incidentally, mostly being either slaughtered or baptised.

When, later, the English were faced with the recurrent Viking threat, from the sack of Lindisfarne in 793 to the invasion which led to the crowning of the Danish Cnut as king of England in 1017, they were reminded that invaders could be instruments of God's wrath. On hearing about Lindisfarne, Alcuin (*c.* 735-804), an English scholar at the court of Charlemagne, claimed that for 350 years the Anglo-Saxons had lived at peace in England, never expecting such a terror. He warned that this dreadful event might have been punishment for sins, some of which he lists – fornication, avarice, wearing pagan hairstyles. Two hundred years later, Wulfstan, archbishop of York (died 1023), took a similar line, referring back to Gildas. Just as the British had brought down the wrath of God for their wickedness, punished by the invasion of the then heathen Anglo-Saxons, so in turn the Anglo-Saxons were being punished for sin by the Viking attacks.

The events of the fifth and sixth century are recorded in documents which had purposes other than objective narrative. They were political and religious propaganda, support for dynastic claims or for the Christian destiny of the Anglo-Saxons and the purposes of God. Most were written centuries after the events they describe, and survive in manuscripts of even later date. They are not straightforward guides even to specific, defined events such as the date, location and outcome of named battles. For the history of population movement, evolution and change they are little more than a possibly misleading sketch.

The Norman conquest brought a radical redirection of British history. The new Norman rulers and their successors had little interest in the history of the defeated Anglo-Saxons, except insofar as they claimed legitimate succession from the Anglo-Saxon kings, especially Edward the Confessor. Not for nothing is Domesday Book divided between record of 'the time of king Edward' and 'now', i.e. 1086. Medieval kings were interested in claiming a classical imperial ancestry, especially through the story of Constantine, whose mother Helena is claimed (on doubtful authority) to have been British. The clearest demonstration of this is to be seen at Caernarvon, where the castle built by Edward I in the late thirteenth century is designed to look like the walls of Constantinople, and in other ways to present Edward as a new Constantine.

It is very clear from the post-conquest histories of Britain how little relevance the ethnicity of the mass of the population may have to accepted national history. There were twelfth-century historians – William of Malmesbury, Henry of Huntingdon – who knew and used the writings of Bede and other Anglo-Saxons, and whose histories are recognisable as such (Gransden 1974). However, the most influential historical work from medieval Britain was Geoffrey of Monmouth's *History of the Kings of Britain*, written in the 1130s, two generations after the Norman conquest. It is still not clear what Geoffrey's sources were, apart from the *Historia Brittonum* and his own imagination, but his influence was considerable. For centuries his version was the one that was read and believed. The detailed chronology of his history is often obscure, but in outline it runs from the Fall of Troy to AD 689, the date Geoffrey gives for the death of his last great British king, Cadwallader. The Anglo-Saxons appear as enemy invaders, returning over many centuries, defeated most definitively by Arthur, and eventually inheriting Britain only after it had been depopulated by plague and emigration. The eventual victory of the Anglo-Saxons was not the result of British defeat but of God's decision. At this point the history ends, presumably with the Anglo-Saxons inhabiting England, but little is made of this.

We find in Geoffrey of Monmouth the fully fledged alternative to the Anglo-Saxon origin myth (MacDougall 1982). This gives the British a classical ancestry – Brutus, great-grandson of Aeneas of Troy, was the founder of Britain. Geoffrey did not invent the idea of Trojan ancestry; it had been claimed in the seventh century for the Franks and appears for the British in the *Historia Brittonum*. The story of Aeneas' escape from Troy and his eventual foundation of Rome – the emperor Augustus claimed ancestry from Aeneas – meant that to claim Trojan ancestry was really to claim a connection with Rome, perhaps even a claim to imperial authority. This certainly appears in Geoffrey of Monmouth's history. He describes how the British, under their great leader King Arthur, fought successfully against the invading Saxons. One intriguing aspect of this story is the relationship between Britain and the Roman empire. Somehow Britain supersedes and is better than Rome – Arthur conquers and rules much of what had been the empire (taking in Norway along the way) and is only recalled from an advance on Rome by news of the treachery of Mordred. This is reminiscent of later nineteenth- and twentieth-century equations of the Roman with the British empire. The Roman empire is the source and model for Arthurian Britain and the Victorian British empire – but in each case the latter is shown as in some subtle way even better than the great exemplar of Rome. Above all of course it was Geoffrey of Monmouth who developed, even if he did not invent, the Arthurian story. The subsequent history of Arthur in story, poem and drama is the history of an important part of British culture, to this day a vital source of inspiration for writers and artists, even though it remains difficult to establish an incontrovertible historical foundation for it. However, for the kings of medieval England Arthur was an ideal ancestor – he was British, with a prior and superior claim to rule than the Anglo-Saxons; he ruled all of Britain, not just England, and much of France; and he was equal, or superior, to the Roman emperors of his day. The succession of the Tudors did nothing to change this, and if he had not died young

Henry VII's eldest son would have succeeded him as a new king Arthur.

Geoffrey tells a story of endless battles between rulers and armies who may be called Briton, Saxon, Roman or even Norwegian, but who do not appear to differ much from one another. Like most early historians, he is interested in the aristocracy, kings and warriors, and has very little to say about ordinary people. He mixes civil war and dynastic conflict with foreign invasions in a way which makes good sense in terms of the history of his own day: the reigns of Henry I, who fought his brother Robert of Normandy, and Stephen, whose reign saw civil war with his cousin the Empress Matilda. Arthur conquered France; William I and his heirs also ruled large parts of France. The time when Anglo-Saxon kings ruled England did not interest Geoffrey or the Norman and Angevin aristocracy. This eclipse of interest lasted for centuries. Old English had become a difficult and unknown language at least by the thirteenth century, if not before. Neither Chaucer nor Shakespeare drew on Bede for their plots. When the Italian scholar Polydore Vergil argued against Geoffrey in his history, written in the reign of Henry VIII, he was reviled as a papist foreigner.

Renewed interest in the Anglo-Saxons came with the Reformation (Graham 2000). Some of the reformers believed that a model for the Church of England could be found in the Church of Bede. So it could be argued that rather than setting out on new uncharted territory the Protestant Church of England was returning to its pure and incorrupt state. There were objectors who pointed out Bede's acceptance of papal authority, and it required very special pleading to equate Anglo-Saxon and Elizabethan doctrines on transubstantiation, but Queen Elizabeth's archbishop, Matthew Parker, an enthusiastic supporter of the Anglo-Saxon Church, managed to do so. He was also master of Corpus Christi College, Cambridge, and there amassed a collection of Anglo-Saxon manuscripts which is still almost unrivalled – and still at the college. The great monastic libraries had been broken up with the dissolution of the monasteries in the 1540s, so it is thanks to the activities of Parker and others like him that any manuscripts were preserved at all. One of the problems he confronted in studying these manuscripts was the language, which had to be translated from Latin and Old English. Parker and his circle thus began the scholarly industry of translation, editing, and compilation of dictionaries and grammars which continues to this day.

The alignment of England with Protestant Europe from the late sixteenth century strengthened ties with Germany and the Netherlands, as opposed to Catholic France and Spain, which also encouraged research into the Germanic ancestry of the English and their language.

Another strand of interest in pre-conquest England was legal. This soon took on political overtones, as precedents for legal and constitutional decisions were sought in ancient documents, including Anglo-Saxon law codes. In the seventeenth century opposition to the monarchy was supported by reference to what was seen as the constitutional rule of Anglo-Saxon kings. Sir Robert Cotton's library, which included many of the surviving Anglo-Saxon manuscripts that had not gone to Cambridge, stood opposite the Houses of Parliament. James I rightly saw the library as a possible source of sedition, and closed it. For the parliamentarians in Charles I's reign the contrast between the Stuarts and the 'constitutional' monarchy of Alfred was clear: Alfred acted in consultation with his 'witan' or council, whereas Charles dissolved Parliament. Just as the religious reformers claimed to be returning to original purity, so the opposition to the King in the Civil War looked back to earlier authority. By this time it was possible to represent the Normans as invading foreigners, ancestors of the Stuart kings, while the English population as a whole was descended from free Anglo-

Saxon peasants, groaning under the Norman yoke from which they were at last to be liberated.

This was not something the English invented in isolation. German scholars rediscovered Tacitus in the Renaissance, and used his *Germania* as the foundation for their history (Rives 1999). Tacitus (*c.* 56 – *c.* 115) believed the Germans of his day to be indigenous, a distinct nation which had not intermarried with foreigners and had not come from anywhere else. He described the bravery of German men, the chastity of their womenfolk – possibly intending a contrast with his own contemporaries in Rome – their kings who did not have absolute power, and the assembly where decisions were debated by everyone (which probably meant all adult free men). Tacitus was a sophisticated author, and we can see now that not all he wrote need be taken at face value, but his work became accepted wisdom in Germany and was also influential in England. Of course, for it to apply to the English they would need to be descended from Tacitus' Germani. This appeared to be demonstrated both by history – even Geoffrey of Monmouth said the Anglo-Saxons eventually took over the empty and wasted land – and by language. The study of philology as it developed in Germany encouraged the identification, since English could be shown to be a Germanic language. Anglo-Saxon studies also became focussed on language, a relatively quiet academic backwater, pursued by a series of notable but rather lonely scholars including at least one woman, Elizabeth Elstob, whose story is one of frustration since she could not find publishers for her later work.

In the seventeenth and eighteenth centuries the Anglo-Saxon origins of the English appeared to be established, although interest in a classical and an Arthurian past never disappeared. What has been called 'the cult of King Alfred' (Keynes 1999) began to offer an alternative heroic king. Keynes has traced the story of Alfred's posthumous rise to fame and fortune via a medieval claim that he founded the university of Oxford, a biography by Spelman, a royalist supporter of Charles I, which did not prevent his adoption as a model of constitutional monarchy, to his Victorian apotheosis as the very model of a Christian king. The extent of his fame in the eighteenth and nineteenth centuries is demonstrated through numerous poems, historical pictures and sculpture, including one on Buckingham Palace. The Victorian pictures – of Alfred and the cakes, Alfred learning to read, Alfred as a minstrel in the Danish camp (Keynes 1999, plates IX-XIV) – have been the models for illustrations in children's history books ever since. It is easy to laugh at a lot of this, but the pictures we see as children form ideas which can be very difficult to dislodge. We probably do not need to dislodge all of it: Alfred does have many achievements to his name, but he was surely not 'the most perfect character in history' as Freeman claimed (Keynes 1999, p. 344).

The Anglo-Saxon people as a whole, not just their most famous king, also became an important part of the political ancestry of the English, because the source of English liberty was seen as deriving from ancient Anglo-Saxon democracy. The Anglo-Saxons were believed to have been ruled by a constitutional king who governed through laws agreed by the assembly of all freemen which were the basis for later English law, and on the advice of his council, the witan. This idea had great influence. It was taken to America by the early settlers, where it remained important. Thomas Jefferson founded the first university department of Anglo-Saxon studies at the University of Virginia as early as 1825. Later, improbably, the southerners defeated in the American Civil War identified with the Anglo-Saxons after the Norman conquest, and foresaw a time when southern civilisation would overcome northern barbarity, as English language and culture had eventually (after some centuries) triumphed over Norman-French (Frantzen and Niles 1997). Anglo-Saxon language and literature in North America have remained important subjects, seen as a significant part of the American cultural heritage.

The most determined proponents of Anglo-Saxon democracy were nineteenth-century historians, some of whom developed what now seem extreme views as to the superiority of the English, especially in contrast to the Celts – whether French or Irish. Implicit in some of these writings was the idea of the English as a separate pure race related to but possibly also superior to the Germans and uniquely fitted to rule other peoples, a convenient imperial myth. There were always writers who doubted that all the Britons had been exterminated, but on the whole this version does imply that most if not all the English were descended from Anglo-Saxon invaders.

Much of this Victorian version of early English history still remains embedded in the subconscious of many English people, re-emerging in school textbooks and television programmes, and still very congenial to some strands of political thinking. Yet throughout the twentieth century it was undermined by contemporary politics, by more critical reading of the historical evidence, and by the enormous increase in archaeological evidence and reappraisal of the significance of that evidence. The nineteenth century saw the start of real archaeological study. Anglo-Saxon burials had been excavated earlier, most notably by Bryan Faussett in the late eighteenth century, who believed them to be of Roman date, although his younger contemporary, James Douglas, correctly identified them as Anglo-Saxon. Serious interest in the subject began with the activities of Victorian antiquarians such as Roach Smith, who published Faussett's finds. However, much of this effort was focussed on excavation, especially of burials, without much critical probing of the historical framework into which the finds from barrows and urns seemed to fit so well. One of the few scholars who tried to integrate archaeological and historical evidence with a critical eye was J.M. Kemble (1807-57), who among other works edited *Beowulf* and wrote a history of the Anglo-Saxons. He had studied philology in Germany and also excavated there (Wiley 1979, p. 237), finding cremation burials which, as he pointed out, bore a striking resemblance to those found in England, thus confirming the connection between the two countries. Support for opposing arguments can be found in his works. His part in strengthening the 'Germanist' school of thought is clear, but his sceptical remarks about early historical sources have also been used in more revisionist approaches. Otherwise the ferment of intellectual activity in the 1860s which inspired the creation of palaeolithic archaeology in the face of accepted biblical chronology almost passed historical archaeology by. The existing historical framework seemed to be uncontroversial, confirmed by archaeological finds which threatened no long-held beliefs.

Since then, archaeological evidence – mostly finds from burials – has been, and continues to be, recovered, recorded and used to illustrate and expand the historical accounts of the Anglo-Saxons. This is still a major focus of research, especially at a local level. Mapping the distribution of burials and artefact types has been the backbone of Anglo-Saxon archaeology for more than a century, as has its interpretation in terms epitomised by E.T. Leeds' early paper, 'The distribution of saucer brooches in relation to the battle of Bedford' (1912). In the middle decades of the twentieth century scholars such as J.N.L. Myres tried to take aspects of Leeds' approach further: archaeological evidence could expand or modify a patchy but nonetheless valid historical record. Pottery could show that Hengest might really have existed, leaving traces of his movements from Jutland to Frisia and Kent (Myres 1948).

For most of the twentieth century, Anglo-Saxon studies were dominated by a few major scholars: H.M. Chadwick, E.T. Leeds, F.M. Stenton and J.N.L. Myres. All were scholarly men who laid the critical foundations of the history and archaeology of Anglo-

Saxon archaeology as it is understood today, even if not all of what they wrote is now accepted. A critical history of the subject would need to explore the biographies of each. Not only were they not themselves immune to contemporary ideology, but the elements of their ideas that reached a wider audience were filtered through popular perceptions. These were inevitably affected by the two world wars. From being friends, cousins and allies of the English, the Germans had become their deadly enemy. Instead of the English ruling Britain and an empire, there was an embattled Britain, all of whose people – Saxon and Celt – needed to unite against a foreign enemy. It became much easier to argue that the Britons had not been exterminated by invading Saxons, but had instead survived as a major element in the population even of eastern England. If Britain could successfully resist invasion from Germany in the 1940s, why not in the 440s as well? Careful reading of the written sources and their combination with archaeology provided a new and plausible picture.

Excavation showed that Iron Age hill forts had been reoccupied in the fifth or sixth centuries AD, presumably by local leaders, who continued to import Mediterranean wine. Closer attention to dating showed that for much of the fifth century there was little evidence of Germanic material culture in the south-west of England – or even in the east before the middle of the century. Between official Roman withdrawal and complete Anglo-Saxon control there was a gap, in some regions of many years' duration. This provided a context for a historical Arthur – or several 'Arthur-type figures', shorn perhaps of Round Table and Grail, but still perhaps significant leaders (Alcock 1971).

The next generation of academic archaeologists reacted against the historical approach, and tried to reject 'Beowulf and brooches' in favour of more theoretically based research, aligning Anglo-Saxon archaeology with prehistory rather than history (Arnold 1988; Hodges 1989). In particular, there was a reaction against the idea of mass migration, partly for reasons outlined in the previous section, but also because of changes in the way archaeologists understand the relationship between ethnicity and material culture. The culture historical mode of explanation has always been a simple, easily grasped concept, which fits well with the way history was understood for many centuries. Separate peoples, or sub-groups, have and had in the past different kinds of material culture – distinctive ways of building houses, burying the dead and making pottery. Plotting finds of those types of material shows where each group lived, and movements of people over time. A more sophisticated analysis of the relationship between material culture and society has shown that this simple equation does not work. People adopt new styles of dress and burial for a variety of reasons, and unravelling the causes of change is a complicated task. As Tom Lethbridge said, just because a brooch came from Hanover it does not follow that the person it was buried with also came from there (Lethbridge 1956).

However, the older modes of explanation have not been entirely replaced. Anglo-Saxon archaeology is a subject which is popular with many people who are not academic archaeologists. There is a great deal of material in our museums and more is found constantly by metal-detectorists and archaeologists. The mid-twentieth-century approach to the subject still has considerable appeal – it seems to combine traditional historical accounts with modern archaeological method to give a soundly based detailed story. Teachers and television producers perpetuate this, partly because it is what they learnt themselves at school and also because it is the story told by most of the accessible books on the subject. It is also a practical approach. To get a point across in a way which is memorable and intelligible to a wide audience it needs to be part of a clear, strongly argued story. Nuance, uncertainty and loose ends simply lead to muddle. Attempts to explain that things might not be so simple often end in non-comprehension, and often meet with resistance because traditional ideas of Englishness are still to some extent bound up with the Anglo-Saxons. Since, as I have argued above, scholarship is itself inextricably embedded in the ideology of its own day, it is not surprising that the competing strands of ethnic and national identity in Britain today should have given rise to contradictory versions of its history.

Before looking in more detail at the archaeological evidence and current perceptions of it, I shall try to assess the contributions made by other disciplines to the debate, especially language and biology.

3

Language

The history of language has in recent years often been linked to archaeological and genetic research. The goal for some scholars is to reconstruct family trees for languages, not just for recent periods but extending back into prehistory, perhaps to the first language ever spoken by humans. This seems to be a more than usually contentious academic field, with some scholars dismissing the conclusions of others as at best hypothetical, at worst fantasy, based on nebulous evidence and misguided arguments. Part of the problem is that some linguists and geneticists use oversimplified definitions of 'peoples' and their histories. There is considerable disagreement over the origins and spread of the Indo-European languages, including the Celtic and Germanic languages, and the relationship between languages and peoples. 'Celtic' has itself become a controversial term (James 1998; Sims-Williams 1998b), but less doubt has so far been raised in relation to the concept of 'Germanic' languages or people.

The counter-argument often presented to any doubts about the scale of Anglo-Saxon immigration is the undoubted fact that the English speak English, not Welsh. English is a Germanic language, descended from Old English, the language of the Anglo-Saxons, which replaced the languages previously spoken in the south and east of Britain. Therefore, it is claimed, there must have been large numbers of Germanic-speaking immigrants who replaced the Celtic-speaking Britons and their language. But languages change for other reasons than population replacement. Languages are disappearing today at an increasing rate, a loss of linguistic diversity comparable to the extinction of species which is diminishing biodiversity, often in the same parts of the world (Nettle and Romaine 2000). What is happening is not so much that people are being killed, or even dying out, but rather that their way of life is under threat, and their culture, including their language, is being submerged and replaced. Over several generations, people move from speaking their native language and possibly several other local languages, to adding the new, often western, language as well, and finally to loss of the original language because younger people use only the new one and knowledge of the native language thus dies with the older generation. The scale on which this is happening now is greater than in the past, and it is linked to the overwhelming economic, political and technological power of the developed countries as opposed to small-scale societies. It is the culmination of the process begun in the sixteenth century with the exploration and colonisation of the New World by the Old, the spread of European people and their languages to the Americas and Australia. The scale on which this is happening now and in recent centuries may be new. But language has always been linked to economic, social and political dominance. In order to succeed it has always been necessary to speak the language of the ruling class. This can mean native people taking on the language of their conquerors, or immigrants adopting the language of their new country. We can see this happening in Britain now: older generations of immigrants speak their native language and learn English, but their children sometimes speak only English. Also, more than one language can exist in one country, used by different groups for different purposes, as Latin existed throughout medieval Europe. The extent and manner in which languages relate to, or replace one another varies, so that each situation needs to be considered on its own terms. In order to begin to use language as an argument, we need to see how far we can actually reconstruct both the history of what was spoken and the processes that caused change.

Two key points should be borne in mind when trying to do this for early medieval Britain and Europe. First, we have no direct evidence for the spoken languages of the past. There are no tape-recordings or films. Secondly, the majority of medieval documents are not written in local spoken languages but in Latin, albeit in versions of Latin often strongly influenced by the local vernacular. Latin remained the language of the Church until the Reformation, and of scholarship even later. It was still learnt by most educated Europeans well into the twentieth century.

Our sources for early languages are the written record, mostly produced for specialised purposes by educated professionals: administrators, tax collectors, the army, the Church and the law. Occasional surviving letters, graffiti or brief informal inscriptions are as near as we can get to the language written by ordinary people, and even that is at some remove from their actual speech. Before printing was invented, all documents were manuscripts, each unique, so that our texts have been transmitted through copies of copies of copies. Many are now fragmentary, most exist only in versions written down long after their original composition. Scribes at various stages may have made mistakes or deliberate changes, adding or removing material they considered irrelevant, and sometimes rationalising language or spelling. The task of both historian and philologist is therefore complicated by the need to unravel layers of textual history to get back to the original version before beginning their own analyses.

Languages are influenced by one another, especially when they remain in contact for centuries. Much research has been devoted to literacy in the ancient and medieval worlds (McKitterick 1990), because the relationship between the written and spoken language will be affected by how many of the population can read and write, and the purposes for which the written word is used. There is a great difference between Gildas, an original author entirely at home in late classical Latin, and someone who could scratch his or her own name on a tile – or even simply recognise writing as such. Gildas was surely able to speak Latin, but recognition and use of a few basic Latin words tells us nothing about the speech of the person involved.

In western Europe, for the first five centuries AD, the dominant language, written and spoken, was Latin. However, the empire was never monoglot: Greek was the alternative language of government and culture, especially in the east, and local languages survived in many places, usually much influenced by Latin or Greek. In some parts of the western empire Latin did replace native languages, after centuries during which both were in use. In what is now France, the Gaulish language disappeared, unless traces survive in Breton. The Latin spoken in France evolved into French, and a similar process resulted in the other modern Romance languages, Spanish and Italian. There is still debate as to exactly when written Latin diverged from spoken Romance, and there must have been much regional diversity in late antiquity as in subsequent centuries. It is interesting to consider why the Germanic Franks who conquered France did not impose their language, as the Anglo-Saxons did in Britain. The simple answer might be that there were proportionally far fewer Franks than Anglo-Saxons in relation to the native populations of Gaul and Britain. It was probably more complicated than that. The key difference is the survival of Latin in Gaul as both, initially, the living spoken language of ordinary people and the language of the educated elite who remained to serve new barbarian masters – as one of them, Gregory of Tours, documents. It has been suggested that part of the mechanism that froze written Latin as an ancient dead language was the development of learning among the barbarians: thus Frankish and Anglo-

Saxon scholars learnt Latin as a foreign language with rules to which they adhered, aspiring to pure classical prose, rather than as a formal version of the living languages they spoke at home. At all events, it was clearly the continuing role played by Gallic aristocrats and bishops under Frankish rule which ensured the survival of Latin. The survival of key elements of the institutional infrastructure, effectively through the Church, and the inclusion of the Franks in that system through their conversion to Christianity, ensured that Latin remained the language of government, even if it became increasingly a foreign language to both Romance and Germanic speakers.

In Britain the situation was clearly different. The expansion of English at the expense of Celtic languages during the past millennium has been approximately mapped, although some details can be disputed. This was a long-drawn-out process – the last Cornish speaker is said to have died in 1777, the last Manx native speaker as recently as 1974 (Nettle and Romaine 2000, p. 2). There are now major attempts to stem the tide for Welsh and for Irish Gaelic, but even with the current local political will and power it still seems unlikely that they will really replace English as the main spoken languages in those countries. This linguistic change has not been achieved through population replacement: the Cornish language died out long before the English developed the habit of seasonal invasion of Cornish beaches. Is what happened in the middle of the first millennium AD comparable to the gradual advance of English which can be plotted during the second millennium, or was this a very different process?

Most discussion of this topic depends to some extent on Kenneth Jackson's *Language and History in Early Britain* (1953). This remains the fundamental work in the field, although most people know it primarily from his map of Celtic river names, often republished. In the fifty years since it was published more evidence, mostly in the form of inscriptions, has been discovered, and some of Jackson's conclusions have been contested and modified – for example, whether the Latin spoken in Britain was a distinct, conservative version of the language, as Jackson argued, or not, as more recent research would tend to suggest (Rivet and Smith 1979, pp. 10-28). What is relevant here is the broad picture of replacement of Celtic by Old English, and the chronology of that replacement. For his absolute chronology Jackson turned to the historical and archaeological accounts accepted at the time he was writing, so any revision of these will at the least 'blur the precision' of his dates (Sims-Williams 1994, p. 221). It is essential to try to avoid circularity, and not to use Jackson as an independent source of evidence for absolute chronology, for his dates depend on what was accepted by historians and archaeologists in the 1950s.

The first question to ask is not why the English speak English and not Welsh, but why they do not speak a descendant of British Latin. Unfortunately in Britain we have very few written documents for precisely the period which concerns us – the fifth to seventh centuries – and even for the Roman period there is not really enough to show conclusively whether Latin was widely spoken by the native population. Our evidence is of course very incomplete since most documents would have been written on perishable materials – papyrus, wood, wax tablets.

We can see that Latin was used for more than formal purposes, because the Vindolanda tablets allow a glimpse of informal written communication in Latin at the level of ordinary army officers and their wives (Bowman 1983). But this was the occupying army, not the native population, most of whom, it can be argued, were neither literate nor even necessarily fluent in Latin, even in the third and fourth centuries. The lead curse inscriptions from temples in the south-west – Bath, Uley and others – do show Latin in use at least at the level of whoever was responsible for such texts at a rural temple such as Uley or Pagans Hill. Many of the curses were written by, or on behalf of, individuals with British names (Tomlin 1988, 1993).There are also enough fragments of informal writing to show that knowledge of Latin was widespread and in use at whatever level of society it is that creates graffiti. So far there is minimal, or no, evidence that British was a written language, which is odd, since continental Celtic languages such as Gaulish were written, both in Greek and Latin scripts.

So far the debate seems inconclusive. Even if Latin was widely in use for all kinds of writing, that does not mean it was the first language of the native population, or even spoken fluently by many of them. It is still possible to argue (like Jackson) that it was the language of the elite, of the army, the administration, commerce and the towns, while the mass of the rural population had only limited knowledge and use of it. Otherwise one might have expected a Romance language to have emerged in Britain as it did in France.

In the west of Britain both elite and church survived, the latter at least using Latin. But even there it did not become the basis for the vernacular languages, which remained Celtic, although many Latin words were adopted. It is true that most of the areas where Celtic languages were spoken after the Roman period were either marginal to the empire, like Wales and Cornwall, or had never been part of it, like Highland Scotland or Ireland. Christianity also was only beginning to be established in the west at the end of the Roman period, and owed far less to the formal institutions of the empire than did the Frankish Church, with its urban bishops descended from Gallo-Roman aristocrats. The west does not, therefore, provide a complete model for the possible linguistic history of the parts of Britain which had been most heavily Romanised, in the south and east. This is where Latin would have been most widely in use, and where evolution of a local Romance language might have been expected. But, except for the Severn valley, this is precisely where Anglo-Saxon influence was strongest, and also where we have least trace of the survival of either native elites or the Christian Church, the key transmitters of Latin culture. We have to admit we do not know whether ordinary Britons were fluent in Latin or had only a basic understanding for practical purposes. It is clear that the mechanisms for maintaining Latin as a spoken or a written language were absent from eastern Britain for most of the fifth and sixth centuries until the Church returned with Augustine, and in this Britain differed markedly from the rest of the former western Roman empire. The reason for this could have been that the Britons, and their languages, were overwhelmed by incoming Anglo-Saxons. Or it could be that the reasons for maintaining a knowledge of, and learning, Latin disappeared during the fifth century, along with the rest of the infrastructure of Roman Britain, leaving a population which spoke largely British. In that case, we need to explain the transition from British to English.

This change is often contrasted with the linguistic effects of the Norman conquest. In 1066 a French-speaking elite replaced the native English aristocracy, but not the English language, because the people as a whole survived and so continued speaking their native tongue. By contrast, in the fifth century the complete change of language is thought to imply a substantial change in population. But the example of the Norman conquest is less straightforward than it might seem. French did have a significant influence on English: Chaucer's language is not the same as Bede's. It can be argued that if King John had not lost control of his ancestors' French lands the rulers and aristocracy of France and England, and their language, would have remained all but interchangeable. The role of Latin is again crucial in that it provided a common language of learning, law and the Church throughout medieval Europe. If French had fulfilled this role after the conquest it is perhaps more likely that it would have replaced English.

It is not clear that we can use linguistic change following either the Roman or the Norman conquest as models for or contrasts to the impact of the Anglo-Saxons. Both can be represented as the introduction of a new language at elite level which was not adopted by the population as a whole. But we do not actually know this to be the case for the Roman period, and it needs modification for medieval England.

The direct evidence for early languages in England falls into two groups (as it does for genetics). There is a very small amount of ancient material, very difficult to interpret and not really sufficient as a basis for generalised conclusions, and a great deal of later evidence whose relationship to the past has to be carefully constructed. In this case the ancient evidence is early texts, the later evidence is existing languages and the written evidence for the development of those languages in Britain since the early Middle Ages.

Formal inscriptions, which were written in Latin, are not necessarily a good guide to local native language. The absence of British inscriptions does mean that this language, and those who used it exclusively, did not have the status of Latin, but it does not mean that the British language had disappeared. Post-Roman inscriptions from western Britain continue in the same tradition, mostly taking the form of memorials written in Latin script and language, although some are written in Irish ogham script, and some include Celtic names. These inscriptions have been interpreted as demonstrating sophisticated biblical scholarship on the part of those who designed them (Thomas 1998). Whether or not this argument is followed, it is clear that they give us only limited information about contemporary vernacular language.

In eastern England we lack formal stone inscriptions from the fifth to the seventh century, when they reappear as part of the material culture of the Christian church, again often, though not always, written in Latin. What we do have, however, are a small number of short inscriptions written in runic letters on portable objects – brooches, pots, combs. Where comprehensible these texts are in Germanic languages. The runic script was developed in the Germanic world, possibly in southern Scandinavia, before the second century AD. It derives from the Latin alphabet, and the concept of writing was one which northern Europeans would have acquired through contacts with the Roman empire. Recent popular accounts of runes usually associate them with magic, and some early inscriptions do seem so enigmatic that religious or magical interpretation is plausible. To illiterate people the concept of writing, the transmission of ideas without face-to-face contact or speech, might in itself seem supernatural. But runes were used widely throughout medieval Scandinavia as a practical utilitarian script, and they are found in Anglo-Saxon England as an alternative to Latin script for a variety of uses including Christian memorial stones and coins.

The scattered early inscriptions from Britain consist of single words or short sentences scratched or inscribed on portable objects, mostly found in graves – pots, brooches, sword scabbards (Page 1999). Some are so incomprehensible that they suggest the people who wrote them did not fully understand what they were doing. There are probably many more inscriptions which have not been identified – faint scratches on the back of brooches might easily be lost through corrosion or conservation or simply not seen. Some of the decoration on metalwork and pottery could well include motifs intended as runic: diagonal crosses for example, since X is the runic letter G. The small existing corpus of runic inscriptions does at least demonstrate a widespread occasional use of Germanic language in eastern Britain from the later fifth century.

These inscriptions are unusual in that they are private, almost secret, whereas surviving early writing tends more often to take the form of public statements – like the memorial stones of western Britain or later Scandinavian rune-stones. This might be taken to mean that the early runes did reflect the language of common people rather than that of the elite. However, many occur in the context of burial, and in Denmark in votive deposits, so they could relate to specialised religious practice.

Philologists have tried to use runic inscriptions as evidence for the early history of the Germanic languages. Different letter-forms relate to regional variation, or to sound changes which entailed the creation of new letters. But because the number of readable inscriptions is still small, new discoveries and revised dating can easily undermine earlier conclusions. Few runic inscriptions have been found in northern Germany, but excavation of burials at Fallward, near Bederkesa, has recently produced several unusually well preserved elaborate wooden objects, including a foot-stool with a clearly cut inscription (Schon 1999). Portable objects can be moved. A sacrificed weapon found in a bog in Denmark, and the inscription on it, might have been local – or part of the equipment of an invading enemy from elsewhere. We cannot assume all rune-cutters subscribed to, or followed, consistent conventions, and some are demonstrably incompetent. Several of the objects found in England have produced considerable debate, hinging on the form of single letters and the date of the deposit. For example, the runic letter H can be written with a single or double cross-bar. The latter is associated with west Germanic and found in later Anglo-Saxon inscriptions, the former has been seen as north Germanic. A single barred H forms part of a word cut on an astragalus buried in a cremation urn at Caistor in Norfolk. This burial was dated by Myres to the fourth century, but by most other scholars to the later fifth (Myres and Green 1972). Is it evidence of a northern component among the Anglo-Saxon settlers – or does it belong to a time before the north and west Germanic forms of the letter had become distinct?

The origins of regional linguistic differences within Britain have been attributed to the varying continental origins of different groups of settlers (via such fragments of evidence as the Caistor astragalus) But they might have developed later within Britain (Hines 1997). More inscriptions will be found, and they will provide further evidence about the early use and development of the Germanic languages, but it seems unlikely there will ever be sufficient material of this kind to answer questions about population and language change. The volume of material from Roman Britain is far greater and yet, as seen above, has not yet provided conclusive answers. And it is worth noting that that is all in Latin, the language which is usually argued not to have been the first language of the majority of the population.

The conversion of the Anglo-Saxons during the seventh century brought the reintroduction of Latin and wider literacy. There are inscriptions, written in both Latin and runic script, and in both Latin and Old English, from the late seventh century, but the majority of our written evidence for Old English consists of much later manuscripts, from the tenth or eleventh centuries. We have to use this material with caution as a source for the history of linguistic change in the fifth century. The later sources belong to the time when Wessex had become politically dominant, under Alfred and his successors, so that the West Saxon dialect also dominates. The languages spoken and written in late Anglo-Saxon England were Germanic – Old English with regional variations, influenced by Scandinavian languages in the Danelaw. If we go back to the eighth century, to the writings of Bede and his contemporaries, we have the impression that Old English was universally spoken by the Anglo-Saxons. Odd references to other languages, such as the strange speech spoken by devils in the Fens to Guthlac, confirm this impression. But are we really in a stronger position than in Roman Britain when it comes to assessing what languages ordinary people really spoke? Writing was closely connected to the Church, used for purposes of religion and government. Where events and people are recorded they are mostly to do with clerics and kings. Most of our information is preserved in later documents. As far as direct contemporary evidence is concerned, we have only the runic inscriptions discussed above. In Bede's day, according to his own account, there was a strong demarcation between Briton and Anglo-Saxon. We may assume that meant that each spoke their own language – but it is an assumption which we can neither prove nor disprove. Even if we do accept that, there is still a long period, more than two centuries at least, during which an originally minority intrusive language might have come to replace native British through a variety of processes other than mass extermination.

Place-names are another source of linguistic evidence. The place-names of Roman Britain, as recorded in classical texts, have survived mostly where they were of major forts, towns or rivers which would have been known to soldiers or seamen around the North Sea (Rivet and Smith 1979). Later names come from records dating often centuries after their creation, many occurring first in Domesday Book. This poses problems of reconstruction and dating of the original forms. We know how Roman Eboracum (probably a Latin version of an older Celtic name) has become York, via Saxon Eoforwic and Viking Jorvik, but if we did not have records of those intermediate stages the relationship might not be obvious. Names can change: Derby and Whitby are names given by Danish settlers to places which previously had English names. What is named can be unclear: Domesday Book records names for places which archaeologically have been shown not to have existed as settlements on their later sites in 1086. Patterns of language and of name giving may be long-lived: the Scandinavian element in northern dialects may have continued to produce names ending in '-by' long after the Viking settlement period. Over the long term, names will be created and revised according to prevailing speech patterns, which will obscure earlier patterns. When the names recorded in the earliest Old English documents were collected (Cox 1975) there was a higher percentage of Celtic names than in later lists (although still not very many), suggesting that such names were progressively lost and replaced by English names – as later English sometimes were by Danish. Margaret Gelling has pointed out that even in the western counties of Devon and Shropshire, which are not thought to have been heavily settled by immigrant Saxons, the place-names are overwhelmingly English, not Celtic (Gelling 1993).

It used to be thought that place-names could be used as historical evidence, by plotting 'early' types of name against Anglo-Saxon cemeteries or Roman settlements. The density of both types of site across south and eastern England now seems to be so great that it would be difficult to find an example of any type of place name which does not occur close to one or both. The idea that fifth-century settlers came into an empty landscape which they cleared and colonised, which underlies some older place-name research, has also been discarded.

Jackson's famous map of Celtic river names does show clearly that the frequency of such names increases towards Wales, but decreases the further east you go. If Celtic speakers had survived in the east, more such names should have been preserved. This is a very reasonable conclusion – and there are not many Celtic names among any of the place-names of England, although more have been identified in recent years (Coates and Breeze 2000). Some of the names which do survive are tautologous, such as 'Avon' as a river name, suggesting imperfect communication.

Some names seem to record the existence of distinct groups of British people: Walton, the settlement of the Welsh; Comberton, the settlement of the Cymry. They are usually interpreted as the names of settlements predominantly occupied by identifiably British people within otherwise Anglo-Saxon areas. This would suggest that there were such enclaves, but they were unusual enough to be worthy of note.

Use of the term for Briton, 'walh', has been studied to see what this reveals of the status of these people. They existed in sufficient numbers to necessitate provision in early lawcodes. They were of lower status but nonetheless included free men, not just slaves (Faull 1975). The word was in fact not seen as incompatible with high status, since it forms an element in the names, and so perhaps the ancestry, of several members of Anglo-Saxon royal families in the seventh century: Cenwalh, Merewalh. Another indication of British elements in Anglo-Saxon dynastic descent is the British name of the alleged founding father of the West Saxon dynasty, Cerdic.

In the end, of course, English did replace British, and the process was already probably far advanced by time of the first written records in the late seventh century. Few Celtic words were borrowed into Old English. It is difficult to deny that for the English language to have acquired such dominance it must have been spoken by a dominant element in society, either numerically or politically. But many of the arguments which use the linguistic transition take for granted oversimplified views of language change. In western Britain there was a very long period of change, not accompanied by mass migration, which resulted in English becoming the dominant language of British peoples. In the east we have a longer period than is sometimes appreciated when a similar process could have taken place, when surviving native British speakers gave up their language in favour of the English speech of their rulers, possibly after a long period of bilingualism and/or regional variation in the speed and scale of change. Our knowledge of this process has been transmitted by educated Christian Anglo-Saxons writing from the late seventh century onwards. They are unlikely to be a perfect guide to the speech of ordinary people during the preceding two or three centuries.

4

Bones, genes and people

The most direct source of information about ancient people is the remains of those people, which usually means their bones. Living descendants can also tell us a lot – if they can be identified.

Different peoples have been distinguished among the populations of Britain, and explained in terms of ancestral migration, since Julius Caesar wrote about them in the first century BC. He contrasted the native people of the interior of Britain with the more civilised inhabitants of the south coast, especially Kent, who he said were descended from Belgic invaders from the continent (*Gallic War* bk V). At the end of the next century, after fifty years of Roman rule, Tacitus had more information about Britain, and describes three peoples (*Agricola* ch. 11). In the north the Caledonians' red hair and large limbs suggested a German origin, while the dark, curly-haired Silures in the west could have come from Spain, but Tacitus was not sure whether the similarity between southern British and Gauls was due to common ancestry or the climate. Other classical and medieval authors named different peoples as inhabiting Britain, usually without much detail, and explained their origins through historical accounts, variously focussed on the peoples they were interested in. These early accounts have had lasting effects: Tacitus' three groups recur in strangely similar form in ancient and modern accounts of Britain. We should at least pause to notice that, five hundred years before the Anglo-Saxon Adventus, the southern British seemed to some observers very like their continental neighbours and unlike other peoples in Britain.

It might be thought that the complexities of historical and archaeological evidence could be avoided by recourse to hard science. Surely direct examination of skeletons or, even better, DNA, will provide clear answers, as newspaper headlines sometimes claim has already happened. A recent review of attempts to distinguish peoples in Britain, however, suggests it is not so simple (Evison 2000).

Physical anthropologists were once confident that it was possible to distinguish races on the basis of the shape of their skull or other skeletal features. For example, John Beddoe's *Races of Britain* (1885) is based on measurements of skulls and variation in the colour of hair and eyes across Britain. Beddoe produced impressive distribution maps which he explained in terms of historical migrations He included illustrations of different physical types – which now all look much more like each other as late nineteenth-century faces than different as Jutes or Britons. There are value judgements in his book – educated men, according to Beddoe, had larger heads than uneducated, and 'the artizan class' was mostly dark-haired. Beddoe's dark westerners, red-haired Scots and tall fair southerners are reminiscent of Tacitus: except that the last are claimed to be descended from Anglo-Saxons, Frisians and Danes, not from Gauls.

Revulsion against misuse of this kind of approach in the twentieth century discouraged research in this area in Europe for many years, and until recently it was rare to find research in Britain which addressed the issue of population change through skeletal analysis. But the idea of clear physical differences between the peoples of Britain is deeply embedded in popular perception and even scholarly research, without very much systematic verification. In cemetery reports, including those written very recently, it has often been claimed that it is possible to distinguish between the taller and more robust skeletons of Anglo-Saxons and the more gracile Romano-Britons. Even their feet are said to be distinctive (Jackson 1995). Similar claims have been made for burials in northern France where at one cemetery, Vron, more robust invading Germanic types were detected (Blondiaux 1993), whereas at another, Frenouville, no invaders were detected, and the same native population was thought to have continued to use the same cemetery while changing its style of grave-goods from Roman to Frankish (Pilet 1980).

There is one modern study in which skull measurements were used as the basis for statistical analysis of variation in early British populations (Brothwell and Krzanowski 1974). This appeared to show little separation between Roman and Saxon in the sample analysed, as opposed to significant difference between Saxon and medieval. A similar unexpected difference around the time of the Norman conquest was detected in a York population, from the cemetery of St Helen on the Wall (Dawes and Magilton 1980). The York result might be explained as the result of repopulation after Norman devastation of the city, but to find such a break more generally in Britain is surprising since the Norman conquest is not thought to have involved replacement of the English population as a whole, only of the aristocracy. Brothwell updated his study in connection with the publication of the burials from Cannington in Somerset (Rahtz et al. 2000). This confirmed that the British and Saxon skeletons in the overall sample were not very different; at Cannington the female skeletons appeared close to Saxon burials, while the males seemed more distinctive. If this had been shown for a cemetery in eastern England it would probably have been presented as demonstrating invading male Saxons and native women. But Cannington is in the south-west, outside any area occupied by Anglo-Saxons during most of the time it was in use (from the fourth century to about 700), and although there might have been invaders from Ireland this should not have affected the late Roman population from the earlier phase of use of the Cannington cemetery. Brothwell concludes his discussion cautiously with the observation: 'evaluation of the Cannington population is thus not easy by osteometric analysis' (p. 177).

There are in fact considerable difficulties involved in identifying ethnicity from bones. The problems are both practical – preservation and availability of skeletons, their representativeness, the choice of measurements and their statistical manipulations – and also theoretical – how to interpret the results. Skeletal growth is affected by nutrition and health, so that even within one family variations in height can exist which are not due to heredity. Modern examples are the growth in size of Americans of Japanese ancestry and the overall increase in stature of recent western populations as a result of changing diet, health and lifestyle, not inheritance. Within past populations the elite may have tended to be taller than the average because of access to more and better food and less strenuous lives than the poor. People who live in towns are subject to more infectious disease and poorer food and living conditions, which can affect growth. Many recorded Romano-British cemeteries are from towns, whereas Anglo-Saxon England was predominantly a rural society. It is possible that like is not being compared with like: poor town-dwellers from the Roman period might have been smaller than Anglo-Saxon warriors, or some other general factor might have encouraged overall growth in British populations from the fourth to the sixth centuries. To make the case for different populations, consistent differences would have to be detected among contemporary burials.

One detailed study of Anglo-Saxon male burials appeared to do this, and to confirm the thesis that stature could indicate ethnic origin. This was the research carried out by Heinrich Härke on Anglo-Saxon burials that contained weapons (Härke

1990). This is an important contribution to Anglo-Saxon archaeology which addresses a major aspect of the evidence, but some of the conclusions have been contested. A large sample of burials containing skeletons osteologically identified as male were divided into those with and without weapons as grave-goods. The first findings of this were that weapons were sometimes buried with boys or men who were too young, too old or too incapacitated to have actually fought with them. Weapons were not therefore simply buried with men of fighting age who had used them in life, but were in some sense a sign of status. This conclusion seems well founded and has been widely accepted. What has aroused more opposition is the next stage of the argument. This is that the two groups, burials with and without weapons, were differentiated in terms of stature. Those with weapons were taller than those without, and, it was further argued, were probably of different ancestry. Weapons appear to have been part of the identity of high-ranking men in early medieval Europe, perhaps especially amongst Germanic societies. It seemed logical to identify the taller skeletons as Anglo-Saxon, the smaller as British, thus arriving at an independently argued demonstration of the distinction noted above as a common unsystematic observation.

This thesis has provoked considerable opposition. Some of this, as Härke has himself wittily recorded in a comparison of English and German reactions (Härke 1998), was to do with the disbelief of German scholars in the survival of any Britons, as opposed to younger English archaeologists' reluctance to accept the arrival of any Anglo-Saxons. But there are also real problems. As with most archaeological research, the sample size is perhaps not large enough to sustain all the conclusions. Explanation in terms of preferential elite nutrition within one population still seems possible, as the evidence Härke presented to counter this has not been universally accepted as conclusive. The expected range of height within one population is in fact greater than the difference observed between the proposed different populations. A study of the women from the same cemeteries as the male burials failed to reveal a similar distinction in stature between those well-equipped with jewellery who might have been expected to be the wives and daughters of the men buried with weapons, and those buried with few or no grave-goods who might have been partners of the non-weapon male burials (Stoodley 1999). It is not possible to hold that the male population could have maintained itself as two distinct groups for several generations if the women were not also distinct – apartheid of this kind is an improbable scenario anyway, especially for communities using the same cemeteries.

One recent researcher addressed the issue through analysis of metrical variation between teeth, which are subject to less environmental influence than other parts of the skeleton (Lloyd-Jones 1997). He measured and compared teeth from burials attributed to Roman and Saxon populations, which showed that in his sample there is more similarity between burials of different dates in the same region, than between burials from different regions. There were no significant differences between 'Roman' and 'Saxon' populations in any one region. Lloyd-Jones argues that for one of his pairs of cemeteries, Berinsfield and Queenford, only 600 metres apart, north of Dorchester on Thames, the burials were 'both derived from the same parent population'. In that case we would have one population using two cemeteries with very different burial rites, since at Queenford few grave-goods were deposited whereas at Berinsfield there was the full range of 'Anglo-Saxon' weapons and jewellery. Berinsfield was a key site in Härke's analysis, which led to the very different conclusion that two populations were using the same cemetery. Another recent PhD thesis (Gowland 2002) includes a comprehensive re-examination of a large number of skeletons from southern England, including Berinsfield and Queensford. This arrives at similar conclusions to those of Lloyd-Jones – that is, that burials from the Oxfordshire and Hampshire cemeteries investigated do not show population change between the fourth and sixth centuries.

Teeth are again the basis for a technique based on stable isotope analysis, which has been used for some time to investigate ancient diet. This is now being used to suggest where an individual might have lived when young – or at least the underlying geology of the region, because this affects the heavy mineral composition of the water which in turn is incorporated into tooth enamel (Montgomery et al. 2000). It can also show that individuals had spent their childhood somewhere other than the place they were buried, thus identifying possible migrants. It would need many successful repetitions of this exercise to demonstrate a large-scale population movement, in future it may become practical to do this. An 'Anglo-Saxon' skeleton from Bamburgh was reported in a British television programme (*Meet the Ancestors*) as having perhaps originated in western Scotland. This is a new technique, with research in progress. If this confirms its potential it might become the most useful technique, because it is relatively cheap and depends on teeth, which are often better preserved than other parts of the skeleton.

Although the studies discussed above may well hold out the best hope of conclusive results in future, another more glamorous scientific field has attracted more attention – and funding – in recent years. Fifty years ago historians hoped archaeologists would answer their questions, now archaeologists look to genetics, the current hope for the solution of all problems, ancient and modern. Press reports encourage the belief that this is all but achieved – one recent headline suggested this book might be unnecessary as geneticists at University College London have proved that the British population was wiped out in the fifth century. Before returning to look at that study in more detail I shall look more generally at the new subject of archaeogenetics, which is, as Colin Renfrew has said, 'a discipline fraught with many pitfalls' (Renfrew and Boyle 2000, p. 4).[1]

There are two ways in which genetics can be used to study the past, using either ancient or modern DNA. Neither is unproblematic. Ancient DNA can be, and has been, extracted from ancient bones. Notable successes, at opposite chronological extremes, include the identification of the skeletons of the last Tsar of Russia and his family, and the demonstration that Neanderthals were genetically distinct from modern humans. However, it has often proved very difficult to substantiate or to replicate results. One difficulty is contamination by modern DNA. Whereas a human scientist who recovers the DNA of an ancient pig is clearly not replicating his or her own skin, there is more room for doubt with humans studying humans, especially when a European scientist studying earlier, but relatively recent, European human DNA produces plausible results. Another problem is that DNA fragments quickly after death, except in unusual conditions of preservation. Bodies only a few years after death may have little well preserved DNA, although in favourable circumstances it can remain for tens of thousands of years. This happens even if the bone is apparently well preserved: its form may survive better than its molecules (Jones 2001). Many Anglo-Saxon burials come from the sandy soils of East Anglia where bone is in any case very poorly preserved.

So far research in this area seems to have met with limited success: a research project carried out at Oxford has not reported conclusive findings (Richards et al. 1993). Even if DNA were to be successfully extracted, this would need to be repeated for many skeletons to produce meaningful patterns rather than anecdotal evidence. Given good fortune in preservation of bones and choice of samples it might be possible to show that an individual buried in England with 'Anglo-Saxon' grave-goods was, or was not, a close relation of someone buried in Germany. But numerous samples from all parts of Britain and the continent would need to be successfully identified before real conclusions could be drawn. To work on the scale really required would need resources which are not currently available for this kind of research. Genetics is a fast-moving field and it would be unwise to suggest this is an impossible future scenario, but at present it does not seem realistic.

The alternative, much more widely used, approach looks at the genetic patterning of modern people as the result of past history, since each of us embodies the history of our ancestors in our genes. It has become relatively easy to collect and identify DNA from living people, so that large samples can be used. As research on the human genome advances, the opportunities expand for application to the study of the past. Back-projecting modern genetic patterns allows the construction of diagrams which show relationships, and statistical analysis allows estimation of the chronology of the evolution of those relationships. The remaining studies discussed in this chapter are all based on extrapolation from modern DNA. There is continuing debate on all aspects of this kind of research, but for some questions it already seems to have provided answers – the peopling of the Pacific, for example.

However, so far it has not resolved all the problems connected with European population movements in the past (precisely the subject of the University College research), most notably the extent to which current Europeans are descended from Upper Palaeolithic populations rather than from immigrant Neolithic farming people. This is a much larger problem than the Anglo-Saxon migrations and has received much more attention, but it remains contentious – which should give us pause when addressing the smaller question. One of the problems is the difficulty of interdisciplinary communication, a particularly acute problem here because of the science/arts divide. It is not possible for most geneticists or archaeologists to grasp the technical detail of each other's subjects, and the temptation is simply to accept conclusions, sometimes even relying simply on press reports, not the actual scientific papers, which is usually a mistake. But we can at least try to see what we understand about one another. From an archaeologist's perspective it seems that the interpretation of genetic patterns in terms of population history used to start from assumptions drawn from oversimplified, or even discredited, historical accounts or archaeological models. More recent studies have more sophisticated historical frameworks, and do seem to offer real hope of providing at least partial answers to some of our questions, as long as the conclusions are carefully tested against alternative possibilities.

There are specific problems associated with the differentiation of Anglo-Saxons from Britons through genetics. The scale of the problem is wrong. It is neither large, to be looked at through the analysis of large samples (e.g. the evolution of modern humans, or even the origin of European populations), nor small, like the identification of familial relationships through study of small groups of individuals. It is not a migration into unoccupied territory, nor is it the last movement of people into that area. It was simply one episode – or series of episodes – in the relatively recent population history of part of one large island. Modern genetic patterns are palimpsests which record accumulated past histories. Disentangling which bit of that pattern, if any, relates specifically to events in the fifth century is not straightforward.

The peoples of north-western Europe and the British Isles are all, according to Brian Sykes, descended from seven women who lived between 40,000 and 17,000 years ago (Sykes 2001). The population of Britain can only be traced back about ten thousand years, to the time when the end of the last ice age led to the re-emergence of habitable land. For the first 1,500 years of that time it was part of the European landmass, visited occasionally by small groups of hunters. Even when the Channel had formed it would be a mistake to think no one could cross it – the Mesolithic populations of northern Europe are known for the extent of their exploitation of marine resources, and they were familiar with the coast of the North Sea. Several more millennia passed before sedentary agricultural communities developed. The idea that farming arrived in Europe or Britain with new immigrant people who replaced earlier Mesolithic hunters has, for most archaeologists, been superseded by more complex models involving both population movement and indigenous adoption of new technologies, often over a very long time-scale.

In any case, whether there was significant migration during the Neolithic or not, both Briton and Saxon derive their ancestry from the resultant European population. On the larger scale these are simply not very different populations. Moreover, what we are trying to identify is one specific phase of movement across the North Sea, within a long history of travel of all kinds across that sea. If there are similarities between the peoples on either side of the North Sea, and differences between them and the inhabitants of Wales and other parts of western Britain, those differences could be the results of cumulative processes involving contacts of all kinds facilitated, or obstructed, by geography. In the days before railways or even good roads it was easier to travel by sea from York to Bergen, or from London to Utrecht, than overland from either to Aberystwyth.

A different picture might be achieved according to whether analysis is based on mitochondrial DNA inherited through the female line, or Y chromosomes inherited through the male. Ideally comparison of results from both is needed. A military take-over would have left native women to become wives of invaders, whereas a folk movement would have brought immigrant women as well. The resultant genetic pattern would be different. Results in one unpublished study using MtDNA showed that a pattern derived from a sample from southern and central England did not differ significantly from Welsh or Cornish data but did differ from north-west Germany, in other words that people in the 'Anglo-Saxon' areas of England are not genetically different from those in the 'British' areas, and are mostly not descended from Germanic immigrants (P. Vorster, personal communication). A related study, also using MtDNA, suggested that north-western German populations are close to both Danish and Frisian (Richards et al. 1993), which must make it difficult to distinguish between fifth/sixth-century Anglo-Saxon and ninth/tenth-century Danish settlers in England.

The alternative approach, using Y chromosomes to trace the male line of descent, is complicated by the fact that some men have been far more successful than others in passing on their genes, whereas other lineages have become extinct. It is not even the case that otherwise successful men will always have more descendants. The family tree of the English royal family shows for example that Edward III had so many descendants that probably his genes are shared by many English people today, and certainly were by all the contestants in the Wars of the Roses, whereas Henry VIII (despite multiple wives) had no legitimate grandchildren, and was ultimately succeeded by a descendant of his sister.

Researchers based at UCL have used Y chromosome data to identify a strong Norse component in the population of Orkney, which strengthens the case for the historically recorded Viking take-over of the islands having involved substantial population change (Wilson et al. 2001). However, this research does not address the issues of survival of native women or the impact of possible long-term prehistoric contacts between Orkney and Norway as a possible contributing factor to genetic similarity.

Relatively isolated populations in places like the Orkneys

might be expected to show clearer patterns than regions with more complicated histories. The same project did not show clear patterns of population movement in other parts of Britain, in fact they concluded that, looking at the male line, 'there has been continuity from the Upper Paleolithic to the present', but that there might have been 'some female immigration'. So it was surprising when another group of researchers from the same institution published rather different results (Weale et al. 2002). However, the first paper did not use samples from England, only from Wales and Ireland, whereas the second compared samples taken from men living in two towns in North Wales and five towns across England, so in fact they are not in such direct contradiction as at first appeared. The results showed clear differences between the Welsh and the English. Further comparison with Norwegian and Frisian samples showed the English and Frisian to be 'statistically indistinguishable' . Technical aspects of this research will need to be assessed by other geneticists before these findings should be accepted as incontrovertibly demonstrated, but meanwhile there are several points which deserve discussion.

First, an alternative explanation for difference between the Welsh and English towns might lie in a contrast between possible 'high genetic isolation and drift in some parts of North Wales' (Weale et al. 2002, p. 1012) and far greater mobility within and between English urban populations since towns first developed in the Anglo-Saxon period. The counter to this might be the closeness of the English and Frisian populations in the sample. This, however, might not be so simple. 'Frisian' is a term applied to the people and language of northern coastal regions of both the Netherlands and Germany, including a series of islands which extend up to the Danish border. The 'Frisian' population used in the MtDNA research by Richards et al. came from modern Germany, especially from the island of Fohr off the coast of Jutland, whereas the UCL sample came from Friesland in the Netherlands. There are clear similarities between Frisia and Anglo-Saxon England in both language and material culture. However, there is an obstacle in the way of arguing for a substantial Frisian component in any migrations to England. This is that during the late Roman period it is difficult to find evidence for any people at all in the northern Netherlands (Gerrets 1999; Besteman et al. 1999), let alone a surplus population ready to emigrate to England and replace a British male population which was numbered at the very least in hundreds of thousands.

A more plausible scenario could be that there was immigration to Friesland from the west, from Lower Saxony, during the fifth century. Genetic similarity between England and Friesland would then be explained as the result of contemporary migration from the same parent population. However, if it is also true that German populations are close to Danish, immigrant Anglo-Saxons might, as has often been suggested, be extremely difficult to distinguish from Danish Vikings. And all the English towns used in the research were well within the Danelaw, most of them in the area where there is most density of place names with Scandinavian elements.

The regional basis for the samples is important. Although some of the research referred to in this chapter seems at first to have produced contradictory conclusions, this is mostly because the authors, or more often the press, have generalised too widely on the basis of data which might have only a limited regional basis. If there is one thing which can be agreed, it is the fragmentation of Britain into separate regions, with different histories. Continuity of populations in southern England might have been far greater than in the east, where there is far more archaeological evidence for immigration, so we should expect research based in different regions of England to give us different answers – as currently appears to be the case.

There is also a problem at present in that the samples are

always taken from areas which are already in contention. To discover whether there was a migration from Germany to England, German and English populations have been analysed. But how distinctive are both or either within the larger north-west European population? The Norwegian samples in the most recent research are a partial answer, but I would like to see other European populations brought in as well. How different are the French to English or German populations? The data probably exists, but when framing research projects like this the focus is always on the areas which have already been highlighted as of interest. This might seem the obvious thing to do. But framing a new research project within existing parameters always carries the danger that the old conclusions will inevitably be confirmed. In general, there is a problem in this area of research in that geneticists often (and the press almost always) seem to assume that ethnicity is clearly and objectively definable, whereas social scientists, including archaeologists, have come to see it, as argued in this book, as a more fluid and complex phenomenon.

Another factor which needs to be considered is the argument that immigration to England can be shown by desertion of the Anglo-Saxon homelands. If that desertion had really been so complete as some have claimed, the population which eventually resettled those deserted continental lands would not be the same as that which had gone to England, and there would be no reason to look for relationships between them. The evidence for that desertion however also needs scrutiny, which is the starting point of the next chapter.

5

Across the North Sea

The 'homelands' of the Anglo-Saxons, according to both historical and archaeological evidence, extend from the mouth of the Rhine across what is now the Netherlands, northern Germany, especially Lower Saxony and Schleswig Holstein, and Denmark, especially Jutland. We have accounts of the peoples of these areas from classical authors, notably Julius Caesar and Tacitus. There has been recent debate (Wells 2001) as to how and why the Germani, the Germans, were differentiated from the Celts. This may lie less in any real original difference between two ethnic groups, more in the differentiation between the people within and outside the Roman empire, which we may owe in the first instance to Caesar, for whom a firm boundary between peoples at the Rhine was a useful device.

The real starting point for most discussion is Tacitus' *Germania*. The Roman empire was reasonably well-informed about lands immediately to the east of the Rhine, including modern Germany, although the devastating defeat of Varus in AD 9 (in a location recently identified from archaeological evidence as near Osnabrück) put an end to Augustus' hopes of adding it to the empire. Tacitus had access to information from military sources, and drew on earlier accounts which also probably had reliable foundations. Much of what he records, therefore, need not be doubted. It is however problematic for several reasons.

Tacitus was a highly educated Roman, who wrote his work within established literary conventions – for example, the difference between barbarian and civilised Greek or Roman. Some of the contrasts he draws may be intended to point up the corruption of his civilised contemporaries, using the barbarian Germani to point up his moral ('no one there is amused by vice'). Also, some of his information may have been old when he recorded it. Above all, for our purposes, Tacitus was writing at the end of the first century AD, and cannot be a reliable guide to the situation prevailing three or four hundred years later.

It is a mistake to regard the frontier of the empire as impermeable, with civilisation on one side, trackless forest inhabited by nomadic savages on the other. Archaeological evidence shows that from the last centuries BC in North Sea coastal regions there was a settled agrarian society. During the Roman period large long-lived villages developed, as well as smaller hamlets or single farms. These settlements included substantial buildings, some with accommodation for many cattle, and other ancillary structures – granaries, workshops, stores. There is evidence for hierarchy in the form of larger farmsteads within some settlements, with greater concentrations of objects, including imports. The quantity of Roman objects, especially in southern Scandinavia between the second and fifth centuries AD, shows that there was active contact between the empire and northern Germania, even within areas remote from the frontier. This contact took many forms: military, political, trade, travel by people of all kinds in both directions. Barbarians arrived in the empire as slaves – but also, increasingly, as soldiers. Late Roman armies were not drawn from the citizenry of Italy but from all parts of the empire. Some barbarians reached the highest levels of imperial service, others returned home with wealth and new ideas. Quantities of Roman objects arrived in the North via all these routes, some to be deposited in graves, many also ending in lake or bog deposits. These extraordinary features, where thousands of weapons were thrown into lakes, are the equipment of armies which must have been numbered at least in the hundreds. The interpretation currently favoured is that these were the sacrificed weapons of defeated armies. Their concentration in southern Scandinavia, together with other evidence such as the existence of central places, suggests that political units of some size and complexity had developed here at least. Interaction with Rome was not just at the level of the acquisition of material; ideas also travelled. The concept of writing led to the development of runic script, a form of writing adapted to cutting letters on wood or stone, or incising them on metal. The imperial image on coins and medals was translated into images of northern rulers and gods. It is possible that memories of an early Scandinavian political power lie behind the later accounts of the Scandinavian origins of the ruling dynasties of various Germanic peoples: Goths, Lombards and Jutes (Hedeager 2000).

Further south in Schleswig Holstein and Lower Saxony in Germany, and into the Netherlands, there are less obvious signs of concentration of power, but there are long established settlements and well furnished graves. Burials in this area were predominantly cremations in urns, but inhumation was also practised. Burials excavated at Fallward in Lower Saxony contained well preserved wooden objects of fourth- to fifth-century date, including an elaborately carved chair and two small tables with turned legs, and a whole series of small containers, some carved in fantastic detail. This find gives us an unexpected window into life in a barbarian settlement far outside the Roman empire, and shows it as neither simple nor savage.

It has been argued that all of this ended, or was seriously disrupted, in the fifth century, the explanation being that people were either driven away by climatic deterioration, or attracted by the prospect of new, richer land within the Roman empire. Hence the barbarian invasions which have been seen as bringing the empire to an end. In particular, abandonment of some regions around the North Sea has been explained in terms of migration to Britain.

Archaeological research over the past two or three decades has however shown that the picture is not in fact at all clear. In the first place, absence of evidence is not evidence of absence. People may cease to bury their dead in an easily discoverable and identifiable manner, for example in highly decorated pots or inhumed with jewellery or weapons, and change to less distinctive burial rites. In the archaeological record this can look as if the people themselves have disappeared. In Denmark this seemed to be the situation: maps of burials show dense distributions for the period up to the end of the Roman Iron Age and then a dramatic fall off to almost nothing, picking up again in the Viking period. Settlement evidence appeared to confirm this gap. At Vorbasse in Jutland, a settlement of the Viking period was excavated and then later nearby an earlier one, which seemed to end during the fifth century. But then further excavation found occupation belonging to the 'missing' centuries (Hvass 1988). This settlement is the classic example of a type which is now quite common in Denmark. During the first millennium AD buildings might occupy their sites only for a generation or two before moving – but not very far, simply across into what had been fields or gardens. Over centuries this can cause a village such as Vorbasse to move over a small area, with the separate periods spatially defined. Excavation on a small scale would reveal only part of the sequence – as the initial investigation here did. Only when very large areas are investigated can we begin to argue that all phases of occupation have really been found. Other settlements and artefacts have made it clear that in Denmark there was not a gap in settlement in the migration period – quite the reverse – despite the decline in identifiable burials (Nasman 1998). In Scania a detailed research project in the Ystad region did show some decline in land-use from AD 200 onwards (Berglund 1991, ch. 3.4). This is described as part of a long-term crisis, from AD 300 to 700, which probably did involve decline in population but also saw concentration of settlement into fewer but larger sites.

Further south, in the Netherlands, the situation was different. The Rhine has always been both a frontier and a routeway, and during the first and second centuries AD this brought prosperity to the region. Incursions across the frontier in the third century led to partial withdrawal by Rome and the end of some civil and military settlements. There does seem to be a settlement gap in the Frisian coastal region, north of the Rhine, but it begins in the late third century, not the fifth. Recent excavations at Wijnaldum, a terp or settlement mound, show that 'layers dating to the mid-fifth century immediately overlie layers which can be dated at the end of the third century' (Gerrets and de Koning 1999, 103). In other words, for 150 years there may have been no occupation here. On a terp, which has a limited area, occupation does not move spatially as on the flat Danish sites such as Vorbasse. Instead it is built up, partly to raise houses above encroaching water. So the missing period is not likely to be found next door – it would be in a salt marsh. However, these excavations also showed how difficult it can be to be precise in dating archaeological sequences on a deeply stratified site like a terp. In the course of successive phases of occupation, material is constantly moved, dug up from earlier phases and built into later structures so that, for example, Roman pottery may come from a pit dug in the Carolingian period.

When occupation is again detectable in Frisia, some of the material suggests close links with the Saxon regions to the east. There has long been evidence for connections also with England, both archaeological and linguistic. Current interpretations do not fit a scenario in which large numbers of Frisians left their homelands to settle England in the fifth century: that is the period which sees an increase of occupation in what had been an underpopulated region. An alternative interpretation is that both Frisia and eastern England were occupied by settlers from northern Germany, from what are now Lower Saxony and Schleswig Holstein.

It is in the latter regions that arguments in favour of desertion caused by migration to England remain strongest. Until recently burial evidence played the main role in this discussion.

A large-scale multi-disciplinary project at Flögeln, near Cuxhaven, was designed to reconstruct the settlement history of a small defined region, using both archaeological and environmental evidence. This was very successful and most of the results have been fully published (Zimmermann 1992). It was possible to reconstruct the course of human exploitation from the earliest prehistoric occupation to the present day, including a clear gap in settlement in the migration period, attributed by the author of the environmental report specifically to migration: 'abandoned around the middle of the sixth century when its people presumably emigrated to Britain' (Behre and Kucan 1994, p. 171) . All the discussions based on this research maintain this thesis.

There is no doubt about the high quality of this research and the evidence it presents. The excavations seem to reveal a clear picture: settlement began in the last century BC and continued until some time in the sixth century AD. A new village, Dalem, began in the second half of the seventh century, to be abandoned in turn at the end of the Middle Ages. At one stage in the investigation it seemed that the fifth century was the end date, but then a later phase of the migration period settlement was found, as was the new village at Dalem. On the basis of excavated evidence alone, I would be inclined to doubt the 'gap', expecting that, as at Vorbasse, the missing periods would eventually be found. After all, in 1978 Professor Zimmerman was confident that the latest finds from Flögeln dated to the mid-fifth century and that thereafter the area was uninhabited woodland until the twentieth century. Since then he has extended the earlier settlement by a century and found a completely new one beginning around 700. This is very like the change in interpretation of the sequence at Vorbasse as more periods emerged from the sand, except that there no break in the sequence is now seen, whereas at Flögeln one does still appear, based increasingly on pollen analysis rather than excavation.

The pollen diagrams do indeed show a gap in cereal cultivation and other indications of human activity,[1] followed by regrowth of forest, at a date (based on C14) in the middle of the first millennium AD. The date of the settlement gap is given as lasting from the second half of the sixth century until, according to dating of the earliest pottery from Dalem, the end of the seventh century, whereas the pollen cores, whose dating depends on C14, suggest a longer gap, until around 750 (Behre and Kucan 1994, 157). The discrepancy might simply result from the imprecision of C14 dates, especially for the sixth century where until recently it has been difficult to establish dates reliably within a range of less than a century. Whatever the precise dates, the diagrams do indicate a sharp decline in evidence for human activity in the immediate area of the settlement, and regeneration of forest following on that decline.

How wide an area does this relate to, and to what extent can one reconstruct migration from the abandonment of one settlement area? The author of this report has explored the methodological issues raised by his research (Behre 1986). He notes that only the cores taken close to the excavated settlement site showed clear indications of human activity. Evidence for cultivation may therefore be reflected only very locally in pollen diagrams, so absence of such evidence cannot be widely generalised and used alone to argue for widespread abandonment. Looking at the pollen diagrams from this project, however, it seems that they do not all tell the same story. Some show little evidence for human activity even at times when the settlement was occupied, as noted by Behre. Others, however, do seem to show such evidence, especially the presence of rye, across the 'settlement gap' (Behre and Kucan 1994, figs 45, 46). Taken together they show how variable the pollen record can be even within a small region. The tree regrowth may reflect a wider situation, but even that does not show an entirely consistent picture across all the diagrams.

Emigration is one possible explanation for abandonment of a settlement, but local small-scale movement or decline in population through famine or plague should also be considered. The end of the medieval village of Dalem has not been attributed to emigration to England and that explanation need not be taken as the only one possible for the end of Flögeln.

Population decline around the North Sea seems most dramatically demonstrated through burial sites. Maps of recorded cemeteries in North Germany and Denmark show the same sharp contrast between dense distributions up to, and in some places during, the fifth century, and very sparse ones afterwards. In Denmark this seems not to correspond with settlement development, but in north Germany it appears that both types of site almost disappear.

Close examination of the pattern in some areas has suggested there was a process of concentration – instead of many small cemeteries several very large ones emerged, for example Suderbrarup in Schleswig, and Issendorf south of Stade in Lower Saxony, which continued in use into the sixth century. One cemetery, Schmalstede, appears to have been used mainly in the fifth century, probably as a successor to another, Bordesholm, which is very close by (Bode 1998). Here we have the same phenomenon as at Vorbasse: burials of a later period were found a short distance away from a cemetery which ended in the early fifth century. The same situation might prevail elsewhere, as yet unrecognised, especially if later burials included more inhumations and fewer of the easily identifiable cremation urns.

One response to the evidence for continued occupation in the fifth century is to look at modern studies of migration. These show that this is a long-drawn-out process, with much traffic in both directions. Young adults leave first, leaving children and the old in their homelands – and perhaps returning there themselves in old age. Analysis of the age and sex of the Suderbrarup burials suggested there might be such a pattern there, with more old people from the latest phase. There was certainly some movement of this kind throughout the later Roman period – young men left to serve in the Roman army and then returned, to be buried with their military belts, maps of which show they were arriving in some quantity up to the mid-fifth century (Böhme 1999). If there was a similar departure to England from that time onwards, occupation of the homelands would continue for some time, but dwindle and disappear during the sixth century, as does seem to have been the case in some places. This would explain the considerable overlap which can be seen between English and continental sites. Some of the discussion in the past has appeared to suggest that crossing the North Sea was such an exceptional event that it took the form of large-scale expeditions at defined points of time, so that once a migrant had left home he would never return. In fact, despite the undoubted dangers of sea travel, in the past water was less of a barrier to communication than long overland journeys. Northern peoples have travelled by boat around and across the North Sea since the Mesolithic. Migration would have involved many expeditions, some small, some large, with repeated return trips, as well as, or instead of, any single major event. The material evidence would fit that picture, because similar artefacts, burials and houses remain in use for generations on both sides of the North Sea, demonstrating continuing contact over a long period.

Comparison of material from an English cemetery, Spong Hill in Norfolk, shows many similarities with North German material. The brooches are like those from Schleswig Holstein, whereas the stamped decoration on pottery finds parallels in Lower Saxony. So it is interesting to discover that Issendorf, which is close to the Elbe, the boundary between these two regions, shows a very similar range of material to that at Spong Hill. In fact, a detailed statistical analysis of the pottery from the two sites showed that they were closer to each other than either was to sites from their own regions, which might mean that here we do have an example of direct connection through migration (Weber 1998).

Much of the evidence, whether from excavation, survey, or environmental research, on a large or small scale, and from both sides of the North Sea, suggests a consistent picture. From before the birth of Christ to around AD 200 there is expansion of all kinds of evidence for human activity. Afterwards there is decline, which ends only around 700. In culture-historical terms, this means that the later Roman Iron Age and the migration period were both times of decline and/or restructuring and reorganisation. But this happens in Britain as well as the continent. The rich villas may have had their heyday in the fourth century, but the towns and rural settlements did not. Among recently excavated sites in eastern England many more are Iron Age to early Roman period than late Roman. If the decline was caused by movement across the North Sea during the fifth century, why does it begin at an earlier date in some areas and why is the area which should have shown increase from immigration also affected?

The answer could be partly environmental. The climate seems to have been warmer and drier in the Roman period, then cooler and wetter until the end of the millennium (P. Dark 2000, pp. 27-8), although the climatic indicators summarised by Dark are not entirely consistent on this. The long-term character of this process suggests that it is probably not explicable in terms of the sudden catastrophes – volcanoes, asteroids – which have recently been suggested.

The context in which we should look for explanations of this long-term, widespread process is the interaction of climate and the changing impact of the Roman empire on the peoples within and outside its frontiers. Comparison might be made with the late medieval population collapse, associated with another climatic deterioration and with the Black Death. It has in fact been suggested that there was a serious epidemic in the sixth century, the 'Justinianic plague', but not all the historical sources used to demonstrate this are entirely reliable.

Complete desertion of any area is not conclusively demonstrated, and in some places contradicted. We need to remember that the most extensively excavated and informative settlement sites include marginal places which were abandoned in times of environmental stress, which is why the evidence remains for us to excavate. They do not include the successful settlements in places which remained occupied to become the towns and cities of medieval and modern Europe; our information from these is inevitably fragmentary and incomplete, salvaged from building sites over the past century. The association of any decline in population with movement to Britain is not clearly demonstrable. Instead, the disruption and restructuring of northern European societies, including Britain, can be seen as a long-term process throughout the central centuries of the first millennium AD, possibly both cause and effect of the decline of the Roman empire.

6

Archaeological evidence

The archaeological evidence for the transition from Roman Britain to Anglo-Saxon England has been described and explained many times.[1] Here I shall not attempt comprehensive coverage, but address some key aspects of the evidence.

In outline the story is simple. In AD 410 or soon afterwards Britain ceased to be part of the Roman empire. This is unlikely to have involved the departure of large numbers of 'Romans': some soldiers and some administrators may have left, and replacements would not have been sent. But there may not have been large contingents of troops left in Britain by then, since successive imperial claimants had taken armies across the Channel to support their unsuccessful expeditions. Neither was Britain governed by a large number of foreigners, but rather by its own Romanised elite, most of whom probably remained to become the local leaders and warlords. The basic population had nowhere to go and for a while may have noticed little difference apart from the continuing deterioration of security and the disappearance of mass-produced goods and imports. So there was not an exodus of people, leaving an empty land, although the undoubted insecurity and war, together with probable epidemics and famine, must have diminished the population .

However, in the archaeological record there is considerable change. The material culture characteristic of Roman Britain declines and ceases to be renewed at some time between the mid-fourth and mid-fifth century. Coins ceased to arrive in any quantity after 410 – there were no soldiers to pay, nor were taxes being collected for the imperial government. Local authorities of all kinds probably did exact tax or tribute, but it was no longer paid in coin. The pottery industries declined and went out of business, as presumably did other large-scale industry. Towns may have already been in decline – when this began is much disputed – but certainly by the late fifth century it is hard to find evidence for urban existence. Stone buildings, mosaics, painted plaster, central heating and baths, roads, forts – all these eventually ceased to be rebuilt or maintained, but exactly when this happened is not clear.

At the other end of the fifth century we can see new forms of burial and buildings – cremations in elaborately decorated pots, or inhumations with weapons and jewellery, the traces of timber buildings and pits full of rubbish, animal bones, loom weights and broken potsherds. People were living in scattered farmsteads or larger villages but not in ordered towns. The infrastructure had gone; the Roman provinces had fragmented into many small territories. The source of much of the new material culture can be found across the North Sea, especially in north Germany. The similarity between English and German material has been clear since Kemble (see above, Chapter 2). The conclusion that migration caused the change retains considerable support.

However, this simple replacement of Romano-Britons by Anglo-Saxons has come to be seen as a less self-evident explanation than once it was. The first problem is that of dating. The fifth and sixth centuries sit between two relatively well dated periods, Roman and Middle Saxon. In the Roman period there is a wealth of dating evidence of all kinds: written sources, coins, stratified building sequences, dendrochronology. In the seventh and eighth centuries, with the return of Christianity, there are again written sources, coins, trade and manufacture on a large scale, imported objects, stratified sites, and some structures and burials dated by C14 or dendrochronology. There are still uncertainties and questions to answer, but at least before 400 and after 600 there is some hope of finding reliable dating evidence. In between the situation is different.

There are no locally minted and few foreign coins. Such rare examples as do exist were often used as jewellery and could have been old when buried. The written sources are few and problematic. The more they are subjected to critical analysis, the less they seem to tell us. The excavated sites – burials, scatters of buildings – do not give good stratified sequences. The timber of which the houses were built has usually decayed – so far in this period we have not found the wells and waterfronts which have produced well preserved waterlogged timbers for dendrochronology in Roman and later Saxon or medieval contexts. Radiocarbon dating may become valuable as its precision increases, but this depends on preserved organic material, of which there is little, mostly human bone.

So most of the chronological discussion has depended on typology, the ordering of artefacts in a developmental sequence according to changes of style or form. In broad terms this works – a Roman pot or brooch is different from an Anglo-Saxon one. Today we can tell sixties from nineties style in houses, cars or jeans, and few of us live in our grandparents' houses or use the same equipment as they did. Style in the past may have changed less quickly, and change did not spread as fast from one region to another, but it did change in ways we can measure and observe. But we have far fewer controls on the rate of change than we do when looking at recent decades, so detailed chronologies depend to some extent on subjective decisions. However sophisticated the statistics and computer programmes designed to identify pattern, the choice of the characteristics to be analysed, and the interpretation of the results, cannot be done mechanically and is subject to human bias. Most of this analysis has used metalwork, especially women's jewellery, as both buildings and weapons show less variation. But not all, or even most, of the variety relates to change over time. There are strong regional differences, with women north and south of the Thames tending to wear different types of brooch, jewellery in Kent differing from both. Status is reflected in dress, some much richer and more elaborate than others. On a smaller scale, there are differences in what is buried with people according to age, and also local preferences. Folk costume in Europe from recent centuries varied according to region, or even village, and also according to status, especially of women – whether they were young, old, married or widowed. Thus extracting the details relevant to chronology is not so simple.

There are relative sequences which are broadly agreed – simple cruciform brooches are earlier than very elaborate ones; one style of zoomorphic ornament succeeds another. Also, the development of one kind of artefact can be related to another through their recurrent burial together in graves. But there is still room for much uncertainty, especially since some types of jewellery may have been made for a long time, and any individual artefact can be old or new when buried. Scholars have devoted their lives to unravelling chronology, and still there are uncertainties, especially with regard to the fifth century. German and Scandinavian scholars seem to have had more success in establishing precisely dated sequences than English. It is not clear whether this is because their material really is inherently more orderly, or because they have not allowed for the complexity of the subject, or because English scholars have not yet managed to order their material as it should be (Hoilund-Nielsen 1997).

At present the number of artefacts which can be securely dated to the fifth century is not large, and even those objects might have been buried later. Very few buildings can be shown conclusively to have been built in the fifth century in Britain. If we believe that Britain had any population at this time we have to accept that they were living in a manner which left little archaeological trace – which continued to be the case in the west of Britain for centuries afterwards – or that we have not yet dated our material correctly. The time when the Anglo-Saxon migration is thought to have taken place is precisely the period for which we have the least incontrovertible evidence.

Some scholars have argued that there was not a sudden change, but a long period when an independent Britain fended off the invaders, who arrived in force only late in the fifth century. Roman buildings could have stayed in use, or been rebuilt, long after there are datable coins or pottery to be found. Excavations at Wroxeter have been influential in this argument: there complex but very fragmentary sequences of construction and occupation were detected overlying a layer dated by a late fourth-century coin (White and Barker 1998). Similar slight traces could have been missed elsewhere. Some types of late Roman metalwork seem to have been made in Britain, and these workshops might have continued. Belt-fittings and brooches ornamented in what has been called the 'Quoit Brooch Style', parts of military equipment, have been found chiefly in south-east England (Inker 2000; Suzuki 2000). They could show a continuing military presence in the early fifth century, perhaps local leaders operating as the successors of Roman commanders and demonstrating their status by wearing appropriate insignia.

An alternative approach back-projects the Anglo-Saxons. In this scenario the belt-fittings are evidence for barbarian soldiers, originally employed by the British authorities as protection against assorted enemies, including their own relations (Hawkes and Dunning 1961). These federates then rebel, send for reinforcements and take control, killing or enslaving the British population. While this story has the authority of Gildas, some of the archaeological evidence used to support it is questionable. The late Roman army included many soldiers of barbarian origin, some of whom rose to very high rank – a Vandal, Stilicho, was commander-in-chief and effective ruler of the empire during the minority of the emperor Honorius (who later had him murdered). If, as still seems likely, the elaborate belt-fittings found in Britain and on the continent were part of official military equipment, there is no reason to describe them as 'barbarian', although many barbarians may have worn them as regular soldiers, or as members of allied tribal groups, sometimes called 'foederati'. The distribution of the find-spots of military equipment should be used with caution as evidence for contemporary troop dispositions – many of the objects were old when lost or buried, perhaps with the man they had been issued to, perhaps with someone who had killed the original owner, or a descendant of one of them.

Some of the reasoning used to support the case for archaeological evidence for foederati is illogical. It is very clear that later Germanic craftsmen learnt much from the Roman empire – types of object, techniques, designs and the ideas behind them were all transmitted – which they then developed and transformed into new idioms. There are connections between the ornament on fifth- and sixth-century Germanic metalwork and pottery and Roman pots and belt buckles of the late fourth century, but to argue that the latter are therefore in any sense 'Germanic' is upside-down reasoning, arising from a compartmentalised scholarship in which Anglo-Saxonists saw classical material simply as a source of parallels for their own, to them, more important material, while Romanists did not usually look at later material.

Both these approaches are consistent with accepting the traditional view of substantial Anglo-Saxon migration – they just disagree about when it happened. Both also accept that, to some extent, material culture relates to groups of people. While any one Anglo-Saxon pot might not have contained the remains of someone whose ancestors lived in Germany, by and large the distribution of such pots reflects the area of settlement of such immigrants. Behind this lies the culture-historical framework of archaeological thought within which E.T. Leeds and his followers worked in the first half of the twentieth century, as did prehistorians. Anglo-Saxon archaeology is not separate from the rest of the subject, nor in any way immune to changes in method and theory. Archaeological interpretation has changed, in response to both the considerable increase in information of all kinds generated by new techniques, and the development of theoretical approaches drawn from anthropology.

In the 1960s and 70s practical archaeology distanced itself, from, or even opposed, the theoretical ideas of the 'New Archaeology', but in retrospect they can be seen to have shared many of the same concerns – and the same confidence. More information of all kinds was being discovered and could be systematically recorded and statistically analysed. Patterns would be detectable and explicable in terms of human behaviour. The arguments were about interpretation: the confidence that enough information, logically dissected, would give clear answers to questions about the past was the same. So also was the idea that peoples in the past operated according to rational principles which could be logically worked out. This intellectual position has great appeal and to many still seems the only constructive approach.

Specifically, survey of all kinds, including aerial photography and, more recently, developer-funded excavation, changed estimates of the scale of early settlement and population size. Later prehistoric Britain was a cleared and settled land, without trackless wastes of forest for immigrants to hew their way into. Even the claylands of Cambridgeshire, once thought relatively empty, now produce traces of settlement of Iron Age and Roman date everywhere new houses are built. The density of settlement in Roman Britain was comparable to, or greater than, it was at the time of the Norman conquest, which implies a population of at least the two million estimated from Domesday Book, probably more. Such a population could not lightly have been eliminated by a few marauding pirates. Similarly, environmental research suggests that the middle of the first millennium AD was not a time of dramatic change in the English countryside. Study of the pollen record has produced a variable picture, with some regrowth of woodland in parts of northern England, but other places where farming continued, perhaps changing from arable to less intensive pastoral. Some of the field boundaries seem to have survived from pre-Roman to early modern times. All of this implies a degree of continuity in the exploitation of the countryside which must have involved some continuing farming population. This kind of information combined with mid-twentieth-century impulses towards British unity and the critique of invasion as an explanation for culture change in the past, to encourage reappraisal of the Anglo-Saxon migration, almost to ask whether it ever really happened at all (Hodges 1989; K. Dark 2000).

This doubt has been developed further by the greater application of anthropological thinking in British archaeology and by post-modern disintegration of certainty about anything and everything. It sometimes now seems that academics are speaking a different language not only from the media and their audiences but also from fieldworkers and museum curators. One the one hand Anglo-Saxons are alive and well – they came from Germany as marauding pirates, then settled down and became friendly farmers in turn assaulted by savage Vikings and Normans, surviving nevertheless as the major part of present English population. On the other, almost all the historical and archaeological evidence can be explained away as ideological presentation of an image which disguised the reality of continuing survival of the British

A major reason for the gap in perception between popular and academic accounts of the Anglo-Saxons is their differing approaches to ethnicity and its reflection in the archaeological record. It still seems perfectly obvious to many people not only that there was a dramatic change in material culture from Roman to Saxon, but that the change must have been caused by a dramatic change in population. Stone buildings fell into disrepair and were replaced by timber huts, towns were abandoned, writing and coinage disappeared, neat rows of inhumations were replaced by hand-made pots full of cremated bones. It is undeniable that there was change in many or even most aspects of the material record of fifth-century England. What has become less clear is exactly how that change was caused.

Where once it was understood that peoples had clear identities, defined through historical inheritance and reflected clearly in their material culture, we now see that ethnicity itself is a far more complicated concept. Ethnic groups define themselves, or are defined by others, according to their perceived differences from other groups. While inheritance is always claimed as a defining factor, the role it plays may in reality be less than that of current political and social forces. If it is difficult, and often controversial, to define ethnic groups in the modern world, it is even more difficult to do so for the past. It used to be argued that peoples could be defined by the kinds of houses they lived in, the dress they wore, their mode of burial. From this it followed that plotting different kinds of houses, pots, and so on would show where separate peoples once lived. Change in those patterns probably meant new people had arrived.

However, modern material culture reflects many other aspects of society as well as ethnicity. The distribution of Japanese technology or American Coca Cola says a great deal about the technology and economic power of those two nations, but not about the distribution of people of Japanese or American ancestry. Churches and mosques are built by many different ethnic groups – though in different local styles.

It is of course true that material culture can be and is used by all of us as a symbolic language to reflect and confirm individual identity. Every time we get up and decide what to put on in the morning we are confirming our membership of a specific group or groups, in our own eyes and those of observers, although the social message we convey may be complicated. Wearing a suit may mean the wearer has a 'high status' job – MP, chief executive – or that s/he is presenting a more formal persona for a wedding or an interview, but cheaper versions may also be worn by office workers or shop assistants who are not free to choose their own clothes, and so the 'high status' connotation has begun to change, with the result that wearing informal clothes can now be seen as reflecting the wearer's freedom of choice, hence status.

Group identity, including national identity, also manifests itself visibly. Tourists can often be identified as American, British, French or German not from any obvious physical variation but simply through the choice of cut or colour of their clothes, the way they wear them, how many and what kinds of camera or bag they carry – as well as how they sound or they way they organise their group. It is also true that material culture is used consciously and unconsciously to define political boundaries – hence the frontier post and the different money distinguishing Croatia from Slovenia.

So the basic principles of culture-historical archaeology have real support and should not be entirely discarded. Groups of people do differentiate themselves through aspects of their material culture, and style does change over time. But material culture has, and had in the past, many different structuring principles. The difficulty we face as archaeologists is in understanding which to use in our interpretation, especially given the incomplete nature of our evidence – its partial survival, preservation and recovery.

Too often we take a predetermined path in interpreting our

carefully assembled maps. For example, distributions of Roman and medieval pottery are mostly explained in terms of production, consumption and trade. Sometimes this can be related to specific historical contexts – the movement of black burnished ware from Dorset to Hadrian's Wall to supply the Roman army, or medieval pottery moving from one part of England to another as part of the goods of a family which owned lands in both places. More general processes, such as the export of wine from the Rhineland or Gascony to England, may explain Rhenish storage vessels in eighth-century Ipswich, or French painted jugs in medieval Southampton. But the movement of pottery from north Germany to England in the fifth or sixth centuries is usually interpreted quite differently. In this case the pots are seen as evidence for migration. Here I am not arguing for or against this interpretation – but it is important to realise that most of the time we are not really establishing independent lines of argument but confirming what we already think we know. We do not think there was migration from Dorset to Hadrian's Wall, or from the Rhineland to Middle Saxon England, though clearly some individuals did move since pots do not transport themselves. But we know about the Roman army and the wine trade, which seem to explain our pottery distributions. In the fifth century the concepts of migration and invasion are so deeply embedded in our thinking that they seem to constitute the obvious explanatory mechanism.

What is the archaeological evidence for fifth-century Britain and can it really be explained in any other way than by the traditional story?

Burial

Burials are the largest and best known class of archaeological evidence for this period, as for other periods of the past. Hundreds of cemeteries containing thousands of burials have been excavated or found by chance. They have always seemed to present the clearest evidence for change during the fifth century. Most of the burials recorded from fourth-century Britain are inhumations, with few or no associated objects. Where grave-goods have been found, such as belt-fittings, they have often been interpreted as an indication of a foreign presence. The graves are mostly arranged in orderly cemeteries outside towns. During the fifth century in eastern England a different type of burial occurs: cremations contained in hand-made decorated pots, with the burnt remains of jewellery. Inhumation remained the most common rite in the south, and again replaced cremation in the east as the dominant rite during the sixth century, many of the burials accompanied by objects, mostly jewellery, weapons and containers. The antecedents for the cremations can be seen in northern Germany, where there are many cremations very similar to those found in England. This extends to the detail of the decoration on the pottery and the combination of types of objects put in them. The change in burial rite corresponds well in terms of date and geography with the traditional account of the Anglo-Saxon migration, and few have hesitated to identify cremations and furnished inhumations as the burials of Anglo-Saxon immigrants. Plotting Anglo-Saxon burials therefore ought to show where Anglo-Saxons settled, and looking at such maps in terms of chronology should show the date at which any part of England was settled, in general moving from east to west from the fifth to the seventh century.

But it is not self-evident that change in burials is driven by any one factor rather than a combination of several – the shift from inhumation to cremation in Britain over the twentieth century may have causes which are partly economic (pressure on land, especially in town centres), partly hygienic (repugnance at decaying bodies), but also religious in the broadest sense (declining belief in an afterlife or at least of the continued existence of our bodies in any afterlife, concentration on this life and avoidance of death, leading to a wish to have bodies neatly processed and buried out of sight). And perhaps we prefer to remember our dead through pictures, as they were when alive, not through visits to a grave, especially in a mobile society where we do not live close to the graves of our ancestors. We should not imagine change had any less complex causes in the past.

Burial practice changed more than once in Britain during the first millennium AD, and it was never uniform over the whole country at any one time. The arrival of the Romans did not mark a change in burial practice. Late Iron Age burials include elaborate elite graves and cemeteries of cremations, the bones contained in hand-made pots, sometimes with associated food bones and occasional items of jewellery. Both types of burial continue after the Roman conquest, perhaps as we would expect with the arrival of new rulers without large-scale population change or, at that stage, a new universal religion. During the later Roman period throughout the empire there was a change from cremation to inhumation – without an obvious simple cause. It is easier to argue that Christianity adopted unfurnished inhumation as the burial rite already current in the fourth century at the time it became a tolerated and then official religion within the empire, than to suggest that the change was caused by Christianity at a time when it was a minority cult. Even east-west orientation was not exclusive to Christian burials. We should resist the tendency to project later elements of Christian practice back into the Roman period. Uniformity of burial practice and control of graveyards seems to have become a concern of the Church in England possibly as late as the tenth century (Gittos 2002). Even the hostility to cremation was not there from the start: St Peter was allegedly cremated. The renewal of Christianity in England during the seventh century did not result in a rapid complete abandonment of grave goods, nor was this when most of our churchyards seem to have been founded. Instead this was a period of variety and lack of consistency in burial practice. Only in the late Saxon period was the medieval pattern of unfurnished, east-west inhumations in village graveyards universally established. The Norman conquest, like the Roman, did not bring a change in burial practice.

It has been argued that the difference between, on the one hand, Roman and Norman, and on the other, Anglo-Saxon, is that the first two were military conquests which resulted in change only at the upper levels of society, so that the population as a whole continued its old religious beliefs and practices. The Anglo-Saxons by contrast came in force as settlers as well as invaders, bringing their own practices with them. Another view can be obtained by taking a broader perspective. Cremation and deposition mostly in hand-made pots was a very widespread and long-lived burial practice across Iron Age Europe. Although fourth-century burial in Britain appears to conform to a pattern of extramural unfurnished inhumation, this may represent only the graves of the most Romanised sector of society. Any other burials, following different rites, would probably belong to the poorer members of society, and would not be distinguished by lavish grave-goods, resulting in small scattered groups of burials which, if unfurnished, would be difficult to date. Some bodies were apparently thrown into ditches in the fourth century. A few cremations of late Roman date have been found and there may have been many more. Cremated bones in an organic container – a bag or box – buried in a shallow pit would be unlikely to survive long. We do not really know much about the burial practice of the rural population in fourth-century Britain. It might not have been so different from that of the Anglo-Saxons.

In northern Europe, although cremation was the major rite, some people were also inhumed. Several recently excavated cemeteries in north Germany included inhumations, some well equipped, as well as cremations, dating to the fourth and fifth centuries AD. It remains true that burial ritual in north Germany can be seen as part of a continuing and evolving native tradition from the pre-Roman period to the sixth century or later, whereas the picture in Britain does seem more discontinuous. But we do not have the whole picture in Britain. The practice of furnished burial seems to have arisen inside and outside the empire at around the same time, the later fourth century, and to belong to a period when stress was put on status as manifested in military rank and possession of visible wealth, in death as in life. The burials with weapons found throughout northern Europe in the late fourth/fifth centuries are not necessarily all to be explained as graves of 'Germanic' soldiers, but rather as members of a new and insecure military aristocracy of various ethnic origins including Germanic. Later, similarly, in the sixth century furnished graves, some very rich, can be found from Spain to Sweden. They were the graves of the elites of those countries, many of whom claimed descent from Germanic dynasties, but most of the people they ruled over were probably of local origin. It is possible to interpret Anglo-Saxon burials in the same way, as the graves of the local aristocracy who might have been of mixed British and immigrant ancestry – or even predominantly native. The counter-arguments are that there are far too many of these burials for them all to be elite (which is true), that this flies in the face of both history and language, and that there are other kinds of archaeological evidence which also show migration.

Buildings

Intrusion of new people from the other side of the North Sea seems even more clearly manifest in buildings than in burials. Wood and thatch replace stone, tiles, plastered walls and mosaic floors. The new buildings in England are very like those found on the other side of the North Sea This includes the 'grubenhaus' or sunken-floored building, whose chief feature is a large pit full of rubbish, easily detectable and recognisable even in very limited excavation. Current English interpretation is that the pit was below a suspended floor, like a cellar, rather than the actual living space, and it is clear that all or most of the material within the pit arrived there as redeposited rubbish after the building over the pit had been demolished (Tipper 2000). It does not seem unreasonable to argue that the people who built these very distinctive structures in Germany also introduced them to England, and that they replaced the Roman building tradition with their own.

But the grubenhaus is a curious building type. A similar form of structure is widespread, and long-lived, in eastern Europe, but in the west it has a limited chronological and spatial incidence, mostly dated to the middle of the first millennium AD and occurring around the North Sea, in southern Germany, and sporadically in Scandinavia. It must have been a response to some perceived practical or cultural need, but what? Isolated early examples have been recorded in Sweden, in the Netherlands from the first century AD, and may begin in the third century in Denmark – although at Vorbasse they appear as a new form only in the fifth century. A few have been tentatively identified on Roman-period sites in England. The date of their introduction is not always clear, but the peak of their use everywhere, including England, was from the fifth to the seventh centuries. On German and Danish settlement sites like Vorbasse and Flögeln, this building type comes into use during the life of the settlement and is not interpreted as evidence for migration. In the Netherlands it is seen as intrusive on the latest, fifth century, levels of terp sites. In England it appears in the fifth century, and is seen as part of the immigrant culture package. But one might argue that if the reason for its introduction into Germany, or any other region, was practical – a new form of storage, or response to climate, that might have contributed to its adoption in England also.

The major ancestral building type on the continent, with roots in the Bronze Age, was the 'long house', a narrow aisled structure which often had accommodation for humans at one end and animal stalls at the other. This is a long-lived and practical farm building type, found later in medieval Britain – but mostly in the north and west, not in the Anglo-Saxon areas. There are rectangular timber buildings without pits on Anglo-Saxon settlements, sometimes described as halls – but they did not have stalls at one end and they are not aisled. Most of these buildings survive only as post holes or wall foundation trenches, so we do not have good evidence for their superstructure or functions, but the plans are very consistent. Why was the major continental building type not transferred?

Various explanations have been suggested, all implying some degree of native survival. Stalling animals is not necessary in the milder climate of south-eastern England – but would settlers not have continued traditional practice at first until they discovered it was not necessary? Would they have lightly abandoned their own traditional form of building unless there had been existing farms and farmers to take over and learn from? It is also argued that the continental house form was evolving towards something like the English form, with fewer or no stalls and posts against the walls (Hamerow 1994). However, smaller houses without stalls are very much in the minority on continental sites and the traditional long house seems to have lived on, especially in Denmark where its evolution can be traced in greatest detail (Hvass 1988).

It can be argued that the most dramatic change in building form in Britain took place during the Roman period, not later. The dominant Iron Age building was the timber round house. It took centuries from the Roman conquest for this to be replaced by rectangular structures at the basic rural level – in parts of the west it never was – but in the south-east, by the fifth century, buildings at all levels of society were rectangular. Many ordinary rural buildings of Roman date were not at all elaborate, but were simple rectangular buildings, with stone walls only as footings. These were not so unlike the later Anglo-Saxon 'halls'. The 'Anglo-Saxon' buildings found in England therefore include grubenhäuser, a relatively new continental type of subsidiary farm structure, and simple rectangular timber structures which are more or less similar to any other simple rectangular buildings. They do not include the dominant building of contemporary continental farms, the long house

Ornament – image and ideology

The form, style and ornament of all kinds of artefacts also changed during the fifth century. But there is a less clear break between classical and Germanic than has sometimes been suggested, and it is also in this area that manipulation of material culture for social and ideological reasons can be most clearly argued. Elaborate brooches to clasp cloaks were a sign of high status in the late empire, as can be seen on all forms of pictorial representation (Janes 1996). This ranges from the emperor himself – Theodosius shown on a great silver dish, or Justinian on the mosaic at Ravenna with elaborate round jewelled brooches – to lesser ranking, but still important men – the ivory carving thought to show Stilicho, the attendant figures on the mosaic with Justinian, all shown wearing crossbow brooches. This concept was known beyond the empire, for example the Frankish king Childeric was buried with a gold crossbow brooch. Even the apparently quintessentially barbaric helmet and shoulder clasps from Sutton Hoo are descended from late Roman parade armour. From the late fourth to the seventh century, styles of ornament and types of equipment can be seen to have wide currency amongst elites across north and west

Europe, on both sides of the former frontier, worn by men of many different origins. Attaching ethnic labels to any of this is probably fruitless, and even if it does reflect movement, this is movement of ideas and of warleaders: it says little about populations.

Within the empire local centres produced distinctive variations on more general styles of metalwork, reflecting regional identities which existed long before the central Roman government lost control (Swift 2000). Techniques and motifs were not lost, but evolved and changed over the centuries. Conscious reworking of classical motifs can be detected even at less exalted levels of society, like the scroll pattern found on some types of Germanic brooch (Dickinson 1993). Even the characteristic Germanic animal ornament has its origins partly in the semi-naturalistic animals found on late Roman strap-ends and buckles. Some of this may have been the creation of ornament for its own sake, but much of it seems to embody ideas. The effect that both political ideology and religious belief can have on material culture is seen in the impact of both the Roman empire and Christianity. They achieved their effect through rather different means, but neither involved mass population movement, yet both had dramatic effects on the material culture of the regions with which they came into contact.

Angles, Saxons and Jutes

To what extent can such interpretations be applied to early Anglo-Saxon England? According to Bede, in his famous passage on the origins of the English, they came from three very powerful tribes, the Saxons, Angles and Jutes. He went on to locate the Jutes, from Jutland, in Kent, the Isle of Wight and part of Hampshire; the Saxons, from Old Saxony, he divides into East, South and West Saxons; the Angles, from Angeln (between the Jutes and Saxons) became the East Angles, Middle Angles,

Mercians and Northumbrians. This account was partly a rationalisation of the political situation, and the names of kingdoms and peoples, of Bede's own day. But that must have rested on earlier traditions, and some of the archaeological evidence can be used to support Bede.

In the sixth century jewellery worn by women in East Anglia, the East Midlands and Yorkshire was different from that worn in the upper Thames valley or southern England, which could reflect Bede's divisions between Angle and Saxon. The jewellery worn by Kentish women is very different again, and it does have some parallels with objects found in the Isle of Wight.

The Jutes of Kent are the clearest case of probable manipulation of material culture. Much of the distinctive jewellery worn by women in sixth- and seventh-century Kent is Frankish in character, not Scandinavian. Proximity and possibly close political ties including dynastic links explain this, not migration. There are also Scandinavian types of object: square-headed brooches, most old when buried, and gold bracteates, probably made in Kent (Behr 2000). Earlier discussions suggested more similarities between Kentish and Jutish finds, including pottery (Myres 1948), but more recent excavations in Jutland do not confirm this comparison. A recent discussion concludes that 'there is no evidence of large scale Jutlandic immigration to Kent' but that an elite which did believe its origins to lie in that region perpetuated that dynastic tradition through a few distinctive heirlooms (Sorensen 1999). The 'Jutish' character of Hampshire and the Isle of Wight is likely to derive primarily from political and dynastic links with Kent (Yorke 1989).

The Saxons too are not entirely explicable in terms of migration. The areas which show strongest input of continental Germanic culture of all kinds are in eastern England, not southern. Some of the 'Saxon' kingdoms lay far outside this region and acquired 'Anglo-Saxon' burials relatively late. Inhumation remained the dominant rite, and where cremations did occur they were mostly poorly furnished, often in undecorated pots. Some of the most characteristic brooches, the saucer brooches, were decorated with 'classical' scroll patterns (Dickinson 1993). Settlements have few grubenhäuser. The further west one goes the less substantial 'Germanic' material is to be found, especially before the later sixth century. Records of the West Saxon dynasties survive in versions which have been subject to later manipulation, which may make it all the more significant that some of the founding 'Saxon' fathers have British names: Cerdic, Ceawlin, Cenwalh.

A good case might be made for southern Britain having been taken over by new ruling dynasties, and their attendant followers, with Germanic ancestry but also intermarrying with British elites. Whether the take-over was early and rapid, as perhaps in Kent, or much later, as in the south-west, there need not have been massive immigration. The long trek westwards of the wagon train across the prairie is not a good analogy: this was a settled populated country, whose people might have been disorganised and demoralised but were not at a lower level of technology or social organisation than their attackers, and were too numerous to be easily removed and replaced.

There remains the Anglian region: East Anglia, the East Midlands and Northumbria. The densest concentration of continental material occurs in East Anglia, including thousands of cremation burials. The sources for this do not seem to lie exclusively in Angeln, roughly equivalent to modern Schleswig Holstein. There are certainly very good parallels for many of the finds: miniature objects, cruciform brooches and some kinds of pottery. But there are also features from the 'Saxon' culture of neighbouring lower Saxony, most notably stamped decoration on pots, which hardly ever occurs in Schleswig, but became the dominant decorative style on sixth-century pottery in England. On the continent stamped pottery is 'Saxon' but in England it seems far more 'Anglian', occurring on more than a third of the pottery from any one site in East Anglia or the East Midlands, but far more seldom in the Thames valley or further south. There were no neat 'Angle' or 'Saxon' packages which transferred across the North Sea. Contributions from further north are also apparent, for example wrist clasps (Hines 1993). In fact the typical 'Anglian' woman's jewellery in sixth-century England consists of a necklace of glass and amber beads of types widespread in the Germanic world, Scandinavian wristclasps, and annular brooches whose origin remains debatable but does not seem to be Schleswig Holstein. The 'Anglian' and 'Saxon' regions on the continent and in England are characterised by different types of pots and metalwork, so that the English material cannot be explained simply through reference to continental ancestry. At the very least there has been mixing of traditions on both sides of the North Sea, and choice of which elements to develop or to abandon. It is probably not surprising that such close parallels can be defined between East Anglia and Issendorf, a cemetery almost on the boundary between Schleswig and Saxony (Weber 1998). If one were to take the North Sea area and plot different types of artefact, for example stamped pottery, annular brooches, cruciform brooches and miniatures, they would be seen to have overlapping but not identical distributions, suggesting a range of contacts and relationships.

The complexity of these relationships becomes even more apparent if more unusual and elaborate objects are examined, where some of the design seems explicable best in terms of shared ideas and/or beliefs. An example of this includes three sets of objects, all dated to the fifth or early sixth centuries. These are a wooden chair and footstool excavated at Fallward in Lower Saxony (Schon 1999); cremation pottery from Spong Hill, Norfolk (Hills et al. 1987), and gold pendants from Denmark (Thrane 1993, pl. 1). The Fallward chair, which has been described as a throne, has decoration which includes interlocking swastika motifs, and on the footstool there is a hunt scene and a runic inscription. Among the Spong Hill pots several are decorated with stamped animals and swastika motifs (Hills 1983), there is one runic stamp, a pot with an incised hunt scene very similar to that on the footstool, and a pot lid in the form of a human figure seated on a chair not unlike the one from Fallward (Hills et al. 1987, fig. 53, pl. IX). Here we see ideas transferring from one medium, wood, to another, pottery, in both instances associated with burial. Similar concepts seem to be represented on the pendants known as bracteates which bear images ultimately derived from Roman coins and medallions, probably translated into pagan mythology (Hedeager 1998). Some carry runic inscriptions, bands of stamped decoration, and occasionally show seated figures, all features seen on the wooden chair and the cremation pots – but in this case on small gold pendants.

While the contacts between Lower Saxony and Norfolk shown by the Fallward chair and the Spong Hill pots could be explained in terms of the traditional migration account, this does not work so well for the bracteates. In fact these parallels suggest connections at the level of ideology and religious belief, expressed through a common stock of ornamental motifs. In later centuries other very distinctive iconographic images, created in all media and art styles, accompanied the spread of Christianity in northern Europe. Even if the conversion was not always the peaceful process it has sometimes been presented as, it clearly often involved the movement of only small numbers of people. Distribution maps of cross-shaped pendants or churches are interpreted in terms of the spread of Christian beliefs, not movement of cross-wearing people, whereas in the earlier period maps of cremation burials and cruciform brooches are read in terms of migration. Some at least of the archaeological evidence for that earlier period can also be read as a reflections of shared ideas and beliefs, not necessarily shared ancestry.

7. Conclusion

In this book I have tried to look at the different kinds of evidence which have been used to construct a picture of the transition from Roman Britain to Anglo-Saxon England. This has always been seen as fundamental to the origins of the English as distinct from any other peoples who have lived in Britain, because it was then that new people, the Anglo-Saxons, are believed to have arrived to conquer and to some extent replace the native British inhabitants of the south and east of the country. I have argued that none of the evidence can be interpreted simply, partly because the situation itself was not simple, but also because, however objective we try to be, we are inevitably subject to both academic and ideological bias.

It is very difficult not to predetermine our conclusions by selecting the evidence that fits what we expect – sometimes constructing research projects in such a way that they are almost bound to prove our point. We often suffer from narrowness of perspective: academic, geographical and chronological. Of course we have to work within practical limits, and there is a tightrope to be walked between superficial breadth and narrow depth – but those limits should be flexible, and not drawn so narrowly that we miss key parts of our story. Moving and redefining boundaries gives new insights: for example, recent use of the term 'late antiquity' for the middle centuries of the first millennium AD goes some way towards dissolving the barrier between 'Roman' and 'medieval'. Geographically England needs to be seen in the context of the rest of the British

Isles and also the North Sea region – and beyond. Cross-disciplinary communication is also a balancing act between respect for others' expertise in their own field and critical appraisal of the interface between their work and our own.

Probably most difficult is to stand back from our own ideologically determined position. Over the centuries views about the Anglo-Saxons and the English have changed for reasons other than logical analysis of evidence. Today there are conflicting points of view which relate to where each of us stands in relation to immigration and Europe. On the one hand, a liberal inclusive standpoint encourages the projection of multiculturalism into prehistory. Immigration has always happened; we are a mixture and will continue to be so. This would encourage the interpretation which sees some Anglo-Saxon immigration but significant British survival, the modern English as the present phase of an ongoing mixture, and indeed part of a constantly reforming configuration of human population which cannot be separated into distinct races or nations. A very different line of argument inclines us to define and maintain local identities within a greater Europe – or in fact within a homogenising global community. So in place of British we have Scots, Welsh and English, all willing to strengthen their modern perceived and experienced differences by reference to the past.

If we return to the evidence surveyed in previous chapters, to what extent does it tell a clear and consistent story?

The historical sources tell us reliably only two things. First, that during the fifth century AD Britain ceased to be part of the Roman empire and was subject to attack from a variety of peoples, including Saxons. Secondly, that the rulers of the peoples living in eastern and southern Britain by the eighth century, and perhaps before that, believed that they could trace their ancestry back to heroic Germanic leaders from the continent. Almost every other 'historical' detail about Britain between *c.* 400 and 600 is subject to considerable doubt.

Why did later rulers believe in, or claim, Germanic ancestry? And should we accept their claims? We do not accept their claims to descent from Caesar, Woden or Noah, but we do give credence to the Angles, Saxons and Jutes because they fit with what we think authoritative voices have already told us, just as Christian Anglo-Saxon kings may have believed the authorities who gave them a biblical descent. We should ask if our faith is really better founded than theirs. When these stories were first created, a pagan Germanic ancestry was something to be celebrated, a glorious past of victorious leaders who belonged to a lineage which surpassed in prestige the alternative British and Roman ancestries which one would expect native British dynasties to have adopted in the east, if they existed there, as they certainly did in the west. The simplest explanation remains the arrival of successful invaders whose descendants celebrated their genuine Germanic ancestors, together with those of any surviving Britons who would have found it expedient to take on an Anglo-Saxon cultural identity. There is a possible alternative scenario. If a significant centre of power had existed in southern Scandinavia during the migration period, as some of the archaeological evidence suggests, it could have provided the impetus for all North Sea rulers and their peoples to become 'Germanic', as earlier many peoples had become 'Roman'. This idea will be rejected by many of us simply because it does not fit with our preconceived ideas, and has no written authority, but it deserves serious exploration – outside the limits of this book.

Even if we accept the traditional explanation the written sources give conflicting dates for the arrival of the invading Germanic leaders – AD 449 according to Bede, whereas the earliest 'historical' individuals in the genealogies seem to have lived a century later. And they do not provide numbers of their followers or reliable accounts of their local origins. Stories of heroic leaders and kings tell us very little about ordinary people.

The history of language is inextricably bound up with the written sources. In the east (but not western Britain) Latin disappeared as the language of the secular and religious elite, themselves destroyed or transformed, and never evolved into a local Romance language. By the eighth century Germanic dialects were spoken and written in England, whereas in other parts of Britain native British languages developed. But there is very limited evidence for the nature and speed of language change in the initial period of some 250 years. The later spread of English across the whole the British Isles was mostly accomplished through its role as the language of a military, political and economic elite, rather than by population replacement – and it took centuries to complete. It is possible that Germanic languages spoken by an incoming elite spread in the same way across a still mainly British population. This would fit with the elite take-over model which could also be consistent with the historical sources. However it suggests a more organised society than has been envisaged for this period. A network of territories with rulers of different origins and speech is a less effective basis for language change than a state. Religion can play a role in language diffusion, as with Latin, but pagan Germanic religion has not been seen as having the kind of centralised structure which needs a consistent ritual language.

Biological evidence is currently seen as the best hope for definitive answers. The ongoing research in these areas supports that hope, but results are often presented as providing conclusions which are more definitive and of more general application than is really the case. Direct analysis of ancient skeletons will only help to address this question when it has become possible to do it on a scale which will allow the accumulation of large databases. Use of modern DNA involves back projection of modern genetic patterns and depends on assumptions which are not always queried. Choosing to look for a relationship between English and Frisian genes depends on the historical sources which suggest such a link. To show that the pattern identified is meaningful we need to look for it in other places, to see whether this is just part of an overall north-western European pattern or something more distinctive. Geneticists also need to explain to the rest of us how they can distinguish between long-term isolation, the result of geographical, political, social or religious factors, and population movements, as causes for patterns of genetic variation. Studies published so far, taken together, suggest regional variation in the history of population within Britain, with varying degrees of continuity and replacement.

Environmental and archaeological evidence also suggests a complex situation. Some elements of the landscape and its exploitation show continuity, others not. In some regions, for example East Anglia, there is still not enough direct environmental evidence for firm conclusions. Material culture certainly does show change, although possibly not in all aspects, but we can see more clearly the pattern established by the end of the sixth century than the initial process. Many of the changes which took place in Britain can be seen throughout western Europe – a considerable decline in evidence for rural settlement and towns, the end of mass production of pottery and other goods, the appearance of furnished inhumations at the end of the fourth century and then again from the end of the fifth until the seventh centuries, use of zoomorphic ornament on elite metalwork. Other features, especially cremation in decorated pots and also grubenhäuser, have a more limited distribution focused on, but not exclusive to, the North Sea region. If we look only at East Anglia and North Germany it is easy to explain similarity in terms of migration. If put in a wider picture both areas can be seen as involved in the disruption and realignment which was cause and effect of the end of the western empire. In particular, since everywhere, including Britain, the evidence for settlement becomes less, it is not self evident that continental homelands have been abandoned because of migration. It is also not the case that regional variation within England reflects directly continental patterns. People and pots did not move as monolithic blocks from one side of the North Sea to another.

A recent discussion suggested that the Anglo-Saxon migration has been subject to more sophisticated reconsideration than the Scandinavian settlement of England during the Viking period (Trafford 2000). That may be true, but it could also be useful to reverse the comparison. The Viking settlement of parts of England is better recorded than the Anglo-Saxon, and so it is easier to see that this was a long-drawn-out and complex process. From the first raids around 800 until 1066, England and the rest of the British Isles was subject to recurrent attack on every scale from opportunistic pirate raids to full-scale military invasion. The extent to which this resulted in Scandinavian elements in the population of England is still debated, but there was clearly great variation between areas where it was significant and others where it was negligible.

This is a useful model with which to approach the earlier period. The contradictions and uncertainties of the evidence reflect the situation on the ground. In the period 400-600 Britain was fragmented. Some territories retained British leadership, language and culture while others lost it, over varying periods of time, to incoming Germanic alternatives. How this happened is partially answered in principle, if not in precise detail, in the written accounts of leaders and battles. All forms of evidence are consistent with the establishment of an elite whose cultural, and probably biological, ancestry, lay in northern Germany and southern Scandinavia. They took control of eastern Britain, probably piecemeal and over a long period. What that meant in terms of population remains elusive because much of the evidence is interpretable in more than one way. The situation is unlikely to have been the same in all parts of England. In some places new rulers may have displaced only the native elite – and married some of their daughters – while elsewhere they were followed, sooner or later, by many humbler settlers. Not only may the 'English' of Somerset or Hereford be closer to the Welsh in ancestry than to the East Anglians, but the populations of Wessex and Northumbria may have been different from each other long before the Vikings settled in the north.

In the end, the answer is probably that the English never were and never will be homogeneous, and also that they, like other peoples, are not ancestrally defined and divided from other peoples with a precise origin at any one time in the past. Another place to seek the origins of the English of today is now.

Notes

1. Introduction

1. A book by Patrick Geary (2002), which appeared as I was completing this one, discusses the history of European nationalism in recent centuries and its real and/or imaginary relationship with the early medieval period. Much of what he says is relevant both to this chapter and to the rest of the book.

2. Attitudes to Anglo-Saxons

1. See Dumville 1977a for the start of a critical debate on the historical sources. For information on all aspects of Anglo-Saxon England see *The Blackwell Encyclopaedia of Anglo-Saxon England* (Lapidge et al. 1999). An even more comprehensive source of information is the web page of Professor Simon Keynes, Department of Anglo-Saxon, Norse and Celtic, Cambridge. This can be accessed at:
http://www.trin.cam.ac.uk/sdk13/asindex.html
This page contains all kinds of useful and interesting information, including bibliographies on all aspects of Anglo-Saxon England and early medieval Europe, collections of pictures of King Alfred, and links to other relevant websites.

For the history of Anglo-Saxon studies see Lucy 1998, ch. 2, Graham 2000, and Frantzen and Niles 1997.

4. Bones, genes and people

1. I am grateful to Professor Martin Jones, Department of Archaeology, Cambridge, and Peter Vorster and Matt Hurles, McDonald Institute, Cambridge, for discussions of the genetic evidence, and also for letting me have copies of published and unpublished papers.

5. Across the North Sea

1. I am grateful to Alan Clapham, McDonald Institute, Cambridge, for discussing the Flögeln pollen diagrams with me.

6. Archaeological evidence

1. The literature on this is very large. Every specialist working in the field has written one or more papers or books on the subject of the Anglo-Saxon migrations. If I referenced all the works I have consulted or have read in the past, let alone all those written, there would be no space for the text in this book. I list here a selection which is intended as representative rather than inclusive, in chronological order of publication. The bibliographies of each will lead to other works: Leeds 1936; Collingwood and Myres 1936; Hills 1979; Böhme 1984; Arnold 1988; Bassett 1989; Esmonde-Cleary 1989; Hodges 1989; Higham 1992; Scull 1995; K. Dark 2000; Lucy 2002.

Bibliography

Alcock, A. (1971) *Arthur's Britain*. Penguin.

Arnold, C.J. (1988) *An Archaeology of the Early Anglo-Saxon Kingdoms*. Routledge.

Bassett, S. (1989) (ed.) *The Origins of Anglo-Saxon Kingdoms*. Leicester University Press.

Beddoe, J. (1885) *The Races of Britain*. Arrowsmith.

Behr, C. (2000) The origins of kingship in early medieval Kent, *Early Medieval Europe* 9 (1): 25-52.

Behre, K-E. (1986) (ed.) *Anthropogenic Indicators in Pollen Diagrams*. Balkema.

——— and Kucan, D. (1986) Die Reflektion archaeologisch bekannter Siedlungen in Pollendiagrammen verschiedener Entfernung-Beispieles aus der Siedlungskammer Flögeln, Nordwestdeutschland. In K-E. Behre (ed.), 95-114.

——— and Kucan, D. (1994) Die Geschichte der Kulturlandschaft und des Ackerbaus in der Siedlungskammer Flögeln, Niedersachsen, seit der Jungsteinzeit, *Probleme der Küstenforschung im südlichen Nordseegebiet* 21.

Berglund, B. (1991) (ed.) The cultural landscape during 6000 years in southern Sweden – the Ystad Project, *Ecological Bulletins* 41. Lund.

Besteman, J.C., Bos, J.M., Gerrets, D.A., Heidinga, H.A. and De Koning, J. (1999) *The Excavations at Wijnaldum*, vol. 1. Balkema.

Blench, R. and Spriggs, M. (1997) (eds) *Archaeology and Language*. Routledge.

Blondiaux, J. (1993) La présence germanique en Gaule du nord: la preuve anthropologique? A propos des nécropoles de Vron (Somme) et de Neuville-sur-Escaut (Nord), *Studien zur Sachsenforschung* 8: 13-20.

Bode, M-J. (1998) Schmalstede: Ein Urnengräberfeld der Kaiser- und Völkerwanderungszeit, *Offa-Bücher* 78.

Böhme, H. (1984) Das ende der Römerherrschaft in Britannien und die angelsächsische Besiedlung Englands im 5 Jahrhundert, *Jahrbuch des Römisch-Germanischen Zentralmuseums* 33: 469-574.

——— (1999) Sächsische Söldner im römischen Heer. In Über allen Fronten, nordwest Deutschland zwischen Augustus und Karl dem Grossen, *Archäologische Mitteilungen aus Nordwestdeutschland*, Beiheft 26.

Bowman, A. (1983) *The Roman Writing Tablets from Vindolanda*. British Museum

Brothwell, D. (2000) The human biology. In P. Rahtz, S. Hirst and S. Wright, Cannington. *English Heritage Monograph Series* 17.

——— and Krzanowski, W. (1974) 'Evidence of biological differences between early British populations from neolithic to medieval times, as revealed by eleven commonly available cranial vault measurements, *Journal of Archaeological Science* 1: 249-60.

Coates, R. and Breeze, A. (2000) *Celtic Voices, English Places*. Shaun Tyas.

Colgrave, B. and Mynors, R. (1969) (eds) *Bede's Ecclesiastical History of the English People*. Oxford University Press.

Collingwood, R.G., and Myres, J.N.L (1936) *Roman Britain and the Anglo-Saxon Settlements. Oxford History of England I.* Oxford University Press.

Cox, B. (1975) The place-names of the earliest English records, *Journal of the English Place-name Society* 8: 12-66.

Dark, K. (2000) *Britain and the End of the Roman Empire*. British Museum.

Dark, P. (2000) *The Environment of Britain in the First Millennium AD*. Duckworth.

Dawes, J.D. and Magilton, J.R. (1980) *The Cemetery of St Helen-on-the-Walls, Aldwark. The Archaeology of York* 12.1.

De la Bédoyère, G. (1999) *The Golden Age of Roman Britain*. Tempus.

Dickinson, T.M. (1993) Early Saxon saucer brooches: a preliminary overview, *Anglo-Saxon Studies in Archaeology and History* 6: 11-44.

——— and Griffiths, D. (1999) (eds) The making of kingdoms, *Anglo-Saxon Studies in Archaeology and History* 10.

Dumville, D. (1977a) Sub-Roman Britain: history and legend, *History* 62: 173-92.

——— (1977b) Kingship, genealogies and regnal lists. In P.H. Sawyer and I.N. Wood (eds) *Early Medieval Kingship*, 72-104. Leeds University..

——— (1985) *The Historia Brittonum*, vol. 3 *The Vatican Recension*. Boydell.

Esmonde-Cleary, A.S. (1989) *The Ending of Roman Britain*. Batsford.

Evison, M. (2000) All in the genes? Evaluating the biological evidence of contact and migration. In D. Hadley and J. Richards (eds) *Cultures in Contact*, 277-90. Turnhout.

Faulkner, N. (2000) *Decline and Fall of Roman Britain*. Tempus.

Faull, M. (1975) The semantic development of Old English wealh, *Leeds Studies in English* VIII: 20-37.
Frantzen, A.J. and Niles, J.D. (1997) (eds) *Anglo-Saxonism and the Construction of Social Identity*. University Press of Florida.
Geary, P. (2002) *The Myth of Nations: the Medieval Origins of Europe*. Princeton.
Gebuhr, M. (1998) Angulus desertus?, *Studien zur Sachsenforschung* 11: 43-85.
Gelling, M. (1993) Why aren't we speaking Welsh?, *Anglo-Saxon Studies in Archaeology and History* 6: 51-6.
Gerrets, D. (1999) Evidence of political centralization in Westergo: the excavations at Wijnaldum in a (supra-)regional perspective. In T. Dickinson and D Griffiths (eds) The making of kingdoms, *Anglo-Saxon Studies in Archaeology and History* 10: 119-26
——— and de Koning, J. (1999) Settlement development on the Wijnaldum-Tjitsma terp. In J.C. Besteman et al., *The Excavations at Wijnaldum*, vol 1: 73-123.
Gittos, H. (2002) Creating the sacred: Anglo-Saxon rite for consecrating cemeteries. In S. Lucy and A. Reynolds (eds) *Burial in Early Medieval England and Wales*, Medieval Archaeology monograph no. 17: 195-208.
Gowland, R (2002) Age as an aspect of social identity in fourth to sixth century England. University of Durham, unpublished PhD dissertation.
Graham, T. (2000) (ed.) *The Recovery of Old English: Anglo-Saxon Studies in the Sixteenth and Seventeenth Centuries*. Medieval Institute Publications, Kalamazoo.
Gransden, A. (1974) *Historical Writing in England c. 550 – c. 1307*. Routledge and Kegan Paul.
Hadley, D. and Richards, J. (2000) (eds) *Cultures in Contact: Scandinavian Settlement in England in the Ninth and Tenth Centuries*. Brepols
Hamerow, H. (1994) 'Migration theory and the migration period. In B. Vyner (ed.) *Building on the Past*, 164-77. Royal Archaeological Institute.
Härke, H. (1990) Warrior graves? The background of the Anglo-Saxon weapon burial rite, *Past and Present* 126: 22-43.
——— (1998) Archaeologists and migration: a problem of attitude, *Current Anthropology* 39(1): 19-45.
Hawkes, S. and Dunning, G. (1961) Soldiers and settlers in Britain, *Medieval Archaeology* V: 1-70.
Hedeager, L. (1998) Cosmological endurance: pagan identities in early Christian Europe, *European Journal of Archaeology* 1(3): 382-96.
——— (2000) Migration period Europe: the formation of a political

mentality. In F. Theuws and J. Nelson (eds) *Rituals of Power from Late Antiquity to the Early Middle Ages*, 15-57. Brill.
Higham, N. (1992) *Rome, Britain and the Anglo-Saxons*. Seaby.
——— (1994) *The English Conquest*. Manchester University Press.
Hills, C.M. (1979) The archaeology of Anglo-Saxon England in the pagan period: a review, *Anglo-Saxon England* 8:297-330.
——— (1983) Animal stamps on Anglo-Saxon pottery in East Anglia, *Studien zur Sachsenforschung* 4: 93-110.
———, Penn, K.J and Rickett, R.J. (1987) The Anglo-Saxon cemetery at Spong Hill, North Elmham, Part IV. *East Anglian Archaeology* 34.
Hines, J. (1993) *Clasps Hektespenner Agraffen*.Kungl. Vitterhets Historie och Antikvitets Akademien.
——— (1994) 'Philology, archaeology and the adventus Saxonum vel Anglorum. In A. Bammesberger and A. Wollmann (eds) *Britain 400-600: Language and History*, 17-36. Heidelberg University Press.
——— (1997) Archaeology and language in a historical context: the creation of English. In R. Blench and M. Spriggs (1997) (eds) *Archaeology and Language* II: 283-294. Routledge.
Hodges, R. (1989) *The Anglo-Saxon Achievement*. Duckworth.
——— and Bowden, W. (1998) (eds) *The Sixth Century* (Brill).
Hoilund-Nielsen, K. (1997) The schism of Anglo-Saxon chronology. In C. Kjeld-Jensen and K. Hoilund-Nielsen (eds) *Burial and Society*, 71-99. Aarhus University Press.
Hvass, S. (1988) Iron Age settlement. In P. Mortensen and B. Rasmussen (eds) Fra Stamme til Staat I Danmark. *Jysk Arkaeologisk Selskabs Skrifter* XXII: 53-92.
Inker, P. (2000) 'Technology as active material culture: the quoit-brooch style, *Medieval Archaeology* XLIV: 25-52.
Jackson, K. (1953) *Language and History in Early Britain*. Edinburgh University Press.
Jackson, P. (1995) Footloose in archaeology, *Current Archaeology* 144: 466-7.
James, S. (1998) Celts, politics and motivation in archaeology, *Antiquity* 72: 200-9.
Janes, D. (1996) The golden clasp of the late Roman state. *Early Medieval Europe* 5: 127-53.
Jones, M. (2001) *The Molecule Hunt: Archaeology and the Search for Ancient DNA*. Penguin.
Keynes, S. (1999) The cult of king Alfred, *Anglo-Saxon England* 28: 225-356
Lapidge, M., Blair, J., Keynes, S. and Scragg, D. (1999) *The Blackwell Encyclopaedia of Anglo-Saxon England*. Blackwell.

Lapidge, M. and Dumville, D. (1984) (eds) *Gildas: New Approaches*. Boydell.
Leeds, E.T. (1912) The distribution of the Anglo-Saxon saucer brooch in relation to the Battle of Bedford, 571 AD, *Archaeologia* 63: 159-202.
——— (1936) *Early Anglo-Saxon Art and Archaeology*. Oxford University Press.
Lethbridge, T. (1956) Anglo-Saxon settlement in Eastern England: a reassessment. In D. Harden (ed.) *Dark Age Britain: Studies presented to E.T. Leeds*, 112-22. Methuen.
Lloyd-Jones, J. (1997) Calculating bio-distance using dental morphology. In S. Anderson and K. Boyle (eds) *Computing and Statistics in Osteoarchaeology* 23-30.
Lucy, S. (1998) *The Early Anglo-Saxon Cemeteries of East Yorkshire*. BAR 272.
——— (2002) From pots to people: two hundred years of Anglo-Saxon archaeology. In C. Hough and K. Lowe (eds) *Lastworda Betst: Essays in Memory of Christine Fell*, 144-69. Shaun Tyas.
——— and Reynolds, A. (2002) (eds) *Burial in Early Medieval England and Wales*. Medieval Archaeology monograph 17.
MacDougall, H. (1982) *Racial Myth in English History*. Harvest House.
McKittterick, R. (1990) (ed.) *The Uses of Literacy in Early Medieval Europe*. Cambridge University Press.
Montgomery, J., Budd, P. and Evans, J. (2000) Reconstructing the lifetime movements of ancient people, *European Journal of Archaeology* 3(3): 370-85.
Myres, J.N.L. (1948) Some English parallels to the Anglo-Saxon pottery of Holland and Belgium in the migration period, *L'Antiquité Classique* XVII: 453-72.
——— (1969) *Anglo-Saxon Pottery and the Settlement of England*, Oxford University Press.
——— and Green, B. (1972) *The Anglo-Saxon Cemeteries of Caistor-by-Norwich and Markshall, Norfolk*. Society of Antiquaries of London Research Report XXX.
Nasman, U. (1998) The Justinianic era of south Scandinavia: an archaeological view. In R. Hodges and W. Bowden (eds) *The Sixth Century*, 255-78. Brill.
Nettle, D. and Romaine, S. (2000) *The Extinction of the World's Languages*. Oxford University Press.
Page, R.I. (1999) *An Introduction to English Runes*, 2nd ed. Boydell.
Pilet, C. (1980) *La nécropole de Frenouville*. BAR International Series 83.
Pohl, W. (1997) Ethnic names and identities in the British Isles: a

comparative perspective. In J. Hines (ed.) *The Anglo-Saxons from the Migration Period to the Eighth Century*, 7-32. Boydell.

——— (1998) Telling the difference: signs of ethnic identity. In W. Pohl (ed.) *Strategies of Distinction: the Construction of Ethnic Communities 300-800 AD*, 17-70. Brill.

Rahtz, P., Hirst, S. and Wright, S. (2000) *Cannington Cemetery: Excavations 1962-3. Britannia* monograph 17.

Renfrew, C. and Boyle, K. (2000) (eds) *Archaeogenetics: DNA and the Population Prehistory of Europe*. McDonald Institute.

Richards, M., Smalley, K., Sykes, B. and Hedges, R. (1993) Archaeology and genetics: analysing DNA from skeletal remains, *World Archaeology* 25 (1): 18-28.

Rives, J.B. (1999) *Tacitus: Germania*. Oxford University Press.

Rivet, A.L.F. and Smith, C. (1979) *The Place-Names of Roman Britain*. Batsford.

Schon, M.D. (1999) *Feddersen Wierde, Fallward, Flögeln*. Museum Bad Bederkesa.

Scull, C. (1995) Approaches to material culture and social dynamics of the migration period of eastern England. In J. Bintliff and H. Hamerow (eds) *Europe Between Late Antiquity and the Middle Ages*. BAR International Series 617: 71-83.

Sims-Williams, P. (1994) Dating the transition to neo-Brittonic: phonology and history, 400-600. In A. Bammesberger and A. Wollmann (eds) *Britain 400-600: Language and History*, 217-62. Heidelberg University Press.

——— (1998a) Genetics, linguistics and prehistory: thinking big and thinking straight, *Antiquity* 72: 505-27.

——— (1998b) 'Celtomania and Celtoscepticism', *Cambrian Medieval Celtic Studies* 36: 1-35.

Sorensen, P. (1999) A reassessment of the Jutish nature of Kent, southern Hampshire and the Isle of Wight. University of Oxford, D.Litt thesis.

Stoodley, N. (1999) *The Spindle and the Spear: a Critical Enquiry into the Construction and Meaning of Gender in the Early Anglo-Saxon Burial Rite*. BAR 288.

Suzuki, S. (2000) *The Quoit Brooch Style*. Boydell.

Swanton, M. (1996) (ed.) *The Anglo-Saxon Chronicles*. Dent. Paperback edition published 2000 by Phoenix.

Swift, E. (2000) *The End of the Western Roman Empire*. Tempus.

Sykes, B. (2001) *The Seven Daughters of Eve*. Bantam.

Thrane, H. (1993) *Guld, guder og godtfolk*. National Museum, Copenhagen.

Thomas, C. (1998) *Christian Celts: Messages and Images*. Tempus.

Tipper, J. (2000) Grubenhäuser: pitfills and pitfalls. University of Cambridge, PhD dissertation.

Tomlin, R.S.O. (1988) Tabellae Sulis. Roman inscribed tablets of tin and lead from the sacred spring at Bath (the curse tablets). In B. Cunliffe, (ed.) *The Temple of Sulis Minerva at Bath*, 2: *Finds from the Sacred Spring*. Oxford University Committee for Archaeology 16.1.

——— (1993) The inscribed lead tablets: an interim report. In A. Woodward and P. Leach, *The Uley Shrines*. English Heritage Archaeological Report 17: 113-30

Trafford, S. (2000) Ethnicity, migration theory and the historiography of the Scandinavian settlement of England. In D. Hadley and J. Richards (eds) *Cultures in Contact* 17-39. Turnhout.

Weale, M.E., Weiss, D.E., Jager, R.E., Bradman, N. and Thomas, M.G. (2002) Y chromosome evidence for Anglo-Saxon mass migration, *Molecular Biology and Evolution* 19(7): 1000-21.

Weber, M. (1998) Das Gräberfeld von Issendorf, Niedersachsen. Ausgangspunkt für Wanderungen nach Britannien?, *Studien zur Sachsenforschung* 11:199-212.

Wells, P.S. (2001) *Beyond Celts, Germans and Scythians: Archaeology and Identity in Iron Age Europe*. Duckworth.

White, R. and Barker, P. (1998) *Wroxeter: Life and Death of a Roman City*. Tempus.

Whitelock, D. (1968) *English Historical Documents*. vol. 1: *c. 500-1042*. Eyre and Spottiswoode.

Wiley, R.A. (1979) Anglo-Saxon Kemble: the life and works of John Mitchell Kemble. In S.C. Hawkes, D. Brown and J. Campbell (eds) *Anglo-Saxon Studies in Arcuaeology and History* I. BAR British Series 72, pp. 165-254.

Wilson, J.F., Weiss, D.A., Richards, M., Thomas, M.G., Bradman, N. and Goldstein, D.B. (2001) Genetic evidence for different male and female roles during cultural transitions in the British Isles, *Proceedings of the National Academy of Sciences USA*, 978: 5078-83.

Winterbottom, M. (1978) *Gildas: The Ruin of Britain and other Documents*. Phillimore.

Wormald, P. (1983) Bede, the bretwaldas and the origins of the Gens Anglorum. In P. Wormald (ed.) *Ideal and Reality in Frankish and Anglo-Saxon Society*, 99-129. Blackwell.

Yorke, B. (1989) The Jutes of Hampshire and Wight and the Origins of Wessex. In S. Bassett (ed.) *The Origins of Anglo-Saxon Kingdoms*, 84-96.

Zimmermann, W.H. (1992) Die Siedlungen des 1. Bis 6. Jahrhunderts nach Christus von Flögeln-Eekholtjen, Niedersachsen: die Bauformen und ihre Funktionen, *Probleme der Küstenforschung im südlichen Nordseegebiet* 19.

Index

CPSIA information can be obtained
at www.ICGtesting.com
Printed in the USA
LVHW081808281218
602065LV00015B/196/P